The Book *of* Romance

The Book *of* Romance

What Solomon Says About Love, Sex, and Intimacy

Tommy Nelson

THOMAS NELSON
Since 1798

NASHVILLE DALLAS MEXICO CITY RIO DE JANEIRO BEIJING

Published in Nashville, Tennessee, by Thomas Nelson. Thomas Nelson is a trademark of Thomas Nelson, Inc.

Thomas Nelson, Inc. titles may be purchased in bulk for educational, business, fundraising, or sales promotional use. For information, please email SpecialMarkets@ThomasNelson.com.

Library of Congress Cataloging-in-Publication Data

Nelson, Tommy.
The book of romance: what Solomon says about love, sex, and intimacy / Tommy Nelson.
p. cm.
ISBN 10: 0-7852-7471-5 (hc)
ISBN 13: 978-0-7852-7471-1(hc)
ISBN 10: 0-7852-8898-8 (tp)
ISBN 13: 978-0-7852-8898-5 (tp)
1. Bible. O.T. Song of Solomon—Criticism, interpretation, etc. 2. Sex in the Bible. 3. Marriage—Biblical teaching. I. Title.
BS1485.2.N45 1998
248.4—dc21
98-8503
CIP

Printed in the United States of America.
07 08 09 10 11 RRD 5 4 3 2 1

To

Herbert and LaVelle Nelson
Parents who made my growing-up years
happy, loved, peaceful, protected,
disciplined, and positively magic.

Teresa Jo Newman Nelson
The delight of my life and fulfillment
of my dreams—the Shulamite
who let me experience the book I teach.

Contents

Acknowledgments

Thanks to Doug and Carrie Hudson for their confidence and continued faithfulness.

To Jan Dargatz for her expertise, talent, and insights in aiding me in writing.

To the faithful saints of Denton Bible, who served as the initial people to receive the Word of God in the Song of Solomon.

To Dean and Barbara Hancock, who first encouraged me to put this in print.

To Richie and Carolyn Fletcher of Gruver, Texas, who have been continual sources of love, encouragement, guidance, and joy to me and my beloved.

Introduction

Does God Have Anything to Say About Love, Sex, and Intimacy?

Several years ago I was driving down a major street in my city when I noticed one of the girls from our congregation walking on the sidewalk. Actually she was floating, almost gliding along the street as if carried by wings. She had euphoria written on her face. She was in this world, a real person, but she might as well have been a million miles away. And I knew the reason for all this—she was in love.

I called out to her from my car, asking her if she needed a ride. She answered, "No, but thank you. I'll just walk."

She was walking on a cloud, and she wanted to enjoy every step of the journey. I knew exactly how she felt. I've been there.

Several months later while I was preaching, I saw her sitting out in the congregation. Her demeanor shocked me so much that I had to pause in my message for a moment and regather my thoughts. After the service was over, I made my way to her. Her countenance was filled with bitterness, anger, hurt, pain, and grief.

I asked only a couple of questions, but her answers revealed volumes. She and her boyfriend had broken off their relationship, but not before they had fallen into immorality. Her heart was broken. She was sorry, guilt-stricken, angry at him, angry at herself, hurt that she had been deceived, and hurt that she had loved so deeply only to be disappointed and rejected. She felt utterly betrayed, not only by this young man, but also by life in general.

Have you ever experienced what this young woman experienced? Have you ever gone through tears and heartache in your relationship with a person you loved? Have you ever been wounded deep within your being by a sexual encounter?

For many young people I know, issues related to love, sex, and intimacy are a mystery. They almost feel as if the world has a secret about these things that they haven't been told. Certainly they haven't heard much about these issues in church. A sermon on sex? A Bible teaching on romance? A practical Sunday school lesson on love and dating?

I can almost see the smile on your face. "But, Tommy," you are probably saying, "the Bible doesn't have anything to say on such matters! It has a lot of 'thou shalt not's' but no 'this is what thou shalt do's' when it comes to sex."

Ah, but you're wrong. The Bible *does* have a great deal of practical and explicit teaching about love, sex, and intimacy. In fact, one entire book of the Bible is devoted to these very issues!

Do you really think that God would give His beloved creations, man and woman, the wonderful feeling we call romance, an institution as mysterious as marriage, and the marvelous passion we know in sexual intimacy and then not have anything to say about these gifts to us? Do you think God would allow men and women to marry and then toss them a grenade called intimacy and say to them, "Well, just fiddle around a little with this and you'll figure out how to work it"? No, indeed not.

The same God who has given us everything pertaining to life and godliness, the same God who calls us to righteousness, holiness, and a life without compromise, the same God who forgives sin and guides those who seek wisdom, this same God is the foremost expert on your need for romance, your sex drive, and your future or current marriage. Based on what He knows about us and desires for us, He has provided an instruction manual so that we might truly live with the joy and intensity of satisfaction that He created us to experience.

That instruction manual of God is the book of the Bible titled the Song of Solomon or, perhaps in your version, the Song of Songs—eight power-packed, very explicit, and highly practical chapters on the topics of love, sex, and intimacy.

"Why haven't I ever heard about this?" you may ask.

For many people, the Song of Solomon is the mystery book of the Bible. Tucked among the books of the Bible in the section called the Wisdom Literature, the Song of Solomon has the distinction of being the only book of the Bible that seems to have been edited and censured by the Christian church. Most Christians don't read it, don't understand it, and have never heard a sermon from it.

Yet no message could be more needed today. The Song of Solomon is *the* book for this generation, in my opinion.

This book takes a specific couple and gives seven snapshots related to attraction, dating, courtship, sexuality, and marriage. In two of the chapters, we watch the couple fight and resolve their conflict. We see how their devotion deepens the longer they are married. We encounter the entire scope of their romantic and sexual relationship, from their first meeting to their passion within marriage. And all along the way, we see that there is something divine in their union. They both experience desire and passion, and yet their desire is always in the right context and timing. A passionate fire builds between them, and that fire is maintained throughout their relationship.

Don't we all desire to love someone passionately, to be loved in return with the same intensity, and to see this love rekindled throughout the years? The heartening news of the Song of Solomon is that God desires for you to experience this kind of ecstasy and enjoy a long-lasting, satisfying love with a spouse.

"But how detailed can God be in a book of the Bible?" you may wonder.

Very detailed. Very graphic. In fact, downright steamy at times. I once taught this book at the Theta Chi fraternity house at the University of North Texas, and as I began to describe the details in one particular passage, one of the guys on the front row looked down at the open book on his lap, then very slowly closed the book just to make sure that it still said "Holy Bible" on the cover!

The material in the Song of Solomon is more detailed, more challenging, and more exciting than any marriage conference I've ever attended. I've never found a guide to love, romance, and sex that is any more profound or any more applicable to real life.

A young man once asked me, "Well, how much can you trust a book that has been written by a guy who had seven hundred wives?"

My answer was simple. "Hey, who should know better?"

It is very often the person who has been on the opposite side of good who knows the most about good. If you want a songwriter who can tell you how best to praise and worship a merciful and faithful God, who better to get than a guy like David who committed murder and adultery and yet still knew the mercy and forgiveness of God? If you want a teacher who can tell you about the shortcomings of the law compared to God's grace, who better to get than a guy like Paul who helped kill the first Christian martyr and harshly persecuted the church, only to be saved by grace and transformed by the power of God's indwelling presence? If you want a person who knows the most about purity of love, sacrificial love, and lasting love, who better to consult than a guy like Solomon? The song that he gave us is about a holy love, one that is distinct and exclusive from all others in the lives of the two people involved. It is a song about a young woman from a lowly place who fell in love with a prince, and he in turn with her. It is a song about the very essence of a passionate and committed relationship.

There is no other book like it. And there is no more important book for you to read and understand if you have any interest whatsoever in what God thinks about love, sex, and intimacy!

One

Who Are You Looking For?

Song of Solomon 1:1–8

A significant number of international students attend the University of North Texas, which is located in the town where I pastor a church. Through the years, my wife and I have had the opportunity to become acquainted with many international students. We do our best to make them feel at home in our city, explain our culture and customs to them and, as opportunities arise, share with them the gospel of Jesus Christ. As best we can, we answer their questions about the way Americans live and Christians worship.

Several of these international students have registered outright shock at the "barbaric" practice we seem to have of young people choosing marriage partners on the basis of whom they like or love. In their cultures, parents do the choosing based upon rather objective and rigid standards. No young person would be trusted to make a wise decision about something so important as a lifelong mate!

They ask, "Why do these young people think they can make a wise choice about marriage when they haven't been married? Why do they think they are able to choose their own mates when they don't even know who they are themselves, much less who they will become? Why don't they trust their parents, who understand something about marriage and know that beauty is deceitful and charm is in vain?"

In their cultures, a marriage partner is chosen by mature adults based upon the character and virtue of both the individual and the individual's family. A match based upon character and virtue becomes the foundation on which romance is expected to grow over time.

These foreign students have a point, in my opinion. For the most part, their cultures have a better track record on enduring marriages than our culture has.

In our culture we too often become consumed with the heady emotion called romance, and very quickly after marriage, we find that the romance evaporates to reveal two very flawed persons in a difficult world. When we discover that the bright and happy romance has devolved into the drudgery of daily living, and much to our dismay, we discover that our spouses have a shortage of character and virtue, we become discouraged and deeply frustrated, and we too often become divorced before the ink on the marriage license has dried. We are a nation of people quick to fall into romance, and then later, quick to bail out of commitment.

What's wrong about our system of dating and marriage?

The same thing that is so exciting about it: it is based on physical attraction.

TO WHAT ARE YOU ATTRACTED?

Before we get too deep in our look at attraction, let's establish one point: attraction is both permissible and desirable. There is nothing wrong with being attracted to a person. If men were never attracted to women, or women to men, the human race wouldn't continue.

Attraction, especially in our culture, is the first stage of any developing relationship—not only in love, but also in virtually any relationship that is formed once we are adults. If we don't perceive a certain chemistry of being able to get along with another person, we are very unlikely to pursue a relationship long enough to develop a friendship or an ongoing business partnership, much less a marriage.

Attraction is two-tiered, however, and we need to be aware of both tiers before we move beyond attraction into the next phase of a romantic relationship.

Tier One: The Physical (Outward)

The first level of attraction that most people experience is physical attraction. When we like what we see, we tend to want to see more of what we like. Physical attraction goes beyond sight; it encompasses all of the senses. We are attracted by a person's voice and laughter, fragrance and cleanliness, and touch or closeness. If any aspect of the physical is a turnoff to us, there is little chance of a relationship developing, at least on the basis of that encounter.

In the opening verses of the Song of Solomon, we find physical attraction at work: "The song of songs, which is Solomon's. Let him kiss me with the kisses of his mouth—for your love is better than wine" (Song 1:1–2). The woman was immediately and strongly attracted to Solomon. She found him utterly intoxicating, even more so than wine. She wanted to kiss him. Believe me, I've encouraged my wife to memorize these verses in six different versions of the Bible. I want her to think of me in this way always!

The song continues, "Because of the fragrance of your good ointments, your name is ointment poured forth; therefore the virgins love you" (Song 1:3). In Solomon's day, men rarely bathed. They used scented oils and ointments on their bodies, both to keep their skin from drying out in the desert climate of the Middle East and to give a pleasing fragrance to their bodies. We do the same today with our aftershave lotions, colognes, and scented deodorants. There is attraction in fragrance, and the woman was openly complimenting the object of her attraction. She might as well have said, "Hey, you're a good-looking man, very attractive and appealing to me."

But notice another part of that same verse: "Your name is ointment poured forth." Here is the real key to *godly* attraction. The woman was attracted to the man physically and spiritually. She was attracted to his reputation for godliness.

Tier Two: Character and Spirituality (Inward)

The second tier of attraction, much more important than the physical, is based on inner qualities—character and one's spiritual relationship with God. In physical attraction, all of the magnets that draw us to another person are external, readily perceived on the outside. We don't have to think about being physically attracted to another person. We automatically feel drawn to the person. Our response is based largely on intuition and feeling.

In character attraction, however, what draws us to another person is rooted deep on the inside. These signs are more difficult to read and understand at times. We may not automatically feel quickly drawn emotionally to a person of good character. Look at what attracted this woman.

"Your name is ointment poured forth," said the woman. This statement has been translated in some versions as, "Your name is like purified oil."

What does "your name" mean?

It is a direct reference to Solomon's character, virtue, and integrity—all of which flowed from his relationship with God. Purified oil is the first pressing of oil from the olive trees that covered the hills surrounding Jerusalem, where

Solomon lived. The first pressing of oil—the extra virgin olive oil, the purest of the pure—was the oil used in the lampstand that burned day and night in the temple. The first pressing of any olive harvest went for temple use only. That was the firstfruits offering from the olive groves; it was designated solely for the worship of the Lord. Purified oil, therefore, was the best, but even beyond the best, it was the best given to God.

That's what the woman saw and liked as much as she admired and was attracted to Solomon's physical presence. She responded at a deep level to the fact that the man who stood before her was a godly man with a good reputation. His "name" was holy. One's name entails all of one's reputation and character. It is what the person really is. Solomon was a man of integrity to the woman. She stated plainly, "Therefore the virgins love you." In other words, *all* the girls she knew thought Solomon was something special. They *all* were attracted to his physical being and his inner character.

So often today, girls will say about a guy, "He's a real hunk." The question begs to be asked, "A hunk of what?" There is nothing wrong with being handsome and appealing, but the real issue is not whether a man is good-looking but whether a man is looking for what is good in God's eyes. Nothing is more discouraging for a woman than to be married to a man whom she discovers later she would not want as a waiter.

We've all heard the saying, "Beauty is only skin deep." If we respond to a person only on the basis of outer beauty, we get a relationship that is as deep as that form of beauty—which is pretty shallow. We've also heard the saying, "Beauty is as beauty does," or "Real beauty comes from the inside." That's the beauty flowing from a beautiful character. We must get to this second tier of attraction—the tier linked to one's character—if we are to have a sound basis for moving on to other stages of a lasting romance.

Tier-one attraction—the physical—is automatic.

Tier-two attraction—character and the spiritual nature of a person—requires spiritual discernment and an objectivity on our part.

To the woman in the Song of Solomon, it was a wonderful thing for Solomon to be handsome, sweet-smelling, and highly kissable. It was an even more wonderful thing for him to have a godly character. She was attracted to him on both tiers, outward and inward.

A WIFE FOR ISAAC

The Bible tells us that when Abraham was old and "the LORD had blessed Abraham in all things" (Gen. 24:1), Abraham determined that the time had come for him to choose a wife for his beloved son, Isaac. Abraham called his most trusted servant to his side and gave him this command: "I will make you swear by the LORD, the God of heaven and the God of the earth, that you will not take a wife for my son from the daughters of the Canaanites, among whom I dwell; but you shall go to my country and to my family, and take a wife for my son Isaac" (Gen. 24:3–4).

The servant naturally asked Abraham how he was to recognize the right young woman. Abraham responded, "[God] will send His angel before you, and you shall take a wife for my son from there. And if the woman is not willing to follow you, then you will be released from this oath; only do not take my son back there" (Gen. 24:7–8).

Notice Abraham's requirements for selecting Isaac's wife:

She was to be of Abraham's family. In our language today as Christians, we would say, "Your spouse must be from the family of God—a fellow believer, one who truly has committed himself or herself to the Lord."

She was to be willing to act on faith. Abraham made it very clear that Isaac's wife was to leave her family and move to Isaac's location, just as Abraham had once been called to leave his family and move out into the land God showed him. In other words, Abraham wanted Isaac's wife to be a woman who was willing to risk all to follow the directives of the Lord. She was to be a woman who lived out an *active faith.*

The best spouse you can ever hope to have is one who does not claim a nominal relationship with the Lord—someone who goes to church occasionally, perhaps was baptized "way back there as a child," or says he or she believes in God. If the person you choose to marry has such a lukewarm relationship toward the Lord, how lukewarm will that person's love for you become as the years progress?

Choose to be attracted to a person who is living out faith in an active, vibrant way—a true follower and disciple of the Lord Jesus Christ, not just an occasional churchgoer.

She was to be revealed to Abraham's servant by an angel. What does this mean to us? It means that we are to trust God to reveal a spouse to us. If you are not already praying that God will send to you His choice for you as a mate, I strongly encourage you to start praying such a prayer today. Ask God to make very plain to you the person He desires for you to date and to marry. Ask Him to send someone your way.

I heard about a young woman who was in her midtwenties, living in a small town in a fairly isolated area of the United States. She confided to a friend of hers that she was living in a two-horse town that didn't even have two cowboys to ride the horses! She longed to be married but had absolutely no prospects for getting married. She felt at a loss as to where to move or what to do next.

She and her friend began to pray and trust God to send

her a husband. Within a matter of weeks, this woman received a call from a man whom she had met several years previously. He lived more than two thousand miles away. She hadn't had any contact with him for at least five years. When he called, he said, "I really don't know why I'm calling, other than to regain contact with you. You've really been on my mind lately, and I keep recalling that we always seemed to communicate well and that you truly had a heart for God. I need a friend I can talk to and who shares my faith in Christ." Well, this woman and her friend certainly knew why she had been on his mind lately!

The man and woman began to correspond and phone with increased frequency, they visited each other in their respective cities, and six months later they were married. They have been married for nearly twenty years now, have been active in lay ministry, and have a godly home.

I don't know how God will answer your prayer for a godly mate—one to whom you are attracted both physically and spiritually—but I believe that He will provide such a mate for you. Trust God to lead you to that person or to lead that person to you.

She was to have a servant's heart. Let's look at one additional factor that was important in the selection of a wife for Isaac. The servant asked the Lord to give him a sign as to which woman he should approach. He prayed, "Now let it be that the young woman to whom I say, 'Please let down your pitcher that I may drink,' and she says, 'Drink, and I will also give your camels a drink'—let her be the one You have appointed for Your servant Isaac. And by this I will know that You have shown kindness to my master" (Gen. 24:14). The chief servant in Abraham's household knew what type of woman God desired for Isaac: a woman with a servant's heart. Sometimes it takes a servant to recognize a servant. Isaac's wife would not fulfill the role of a servant in Isaac's home, but having a servant's heart is a wonderful quality of character. Such a person is a generous giver, not a greedy taker.

Abraham's servant had traveled more than five hundred miles north to the place where Abraham's relatives lived. He had been given a caravan of ten camels laden with supplies for the journey and gifts for the chosen bride and her family. He was looking specifically for a young woman who would be willing to draw water from a well to satisfy ten camels. Now that's a servant!

A camel can store up to thirty gallons of water in its body. Ten camels, three hundred gallons of water. Each camel was probably not in need of thirty gallons of water, but even if all of them were only "half empty" upon arrival in Haran, where Abraham's family lived, the woman had a great deal of water to draw.

Let me assure you, there is nothing as winsome as a servant's heart in a potential spouse. Is the person to whom you are attracted quick to give to others, quick to go the second mile in serving others, quick to offer assistance, quick to volunteer in the face of a need? Or does the person seem to live only for himself or herself, withdraw from the needs of others, or seek to satisfy only self?

A selfish, do-for-me-and-don't-ask-me-to-do-for-you person is *not* someone with whom you will be happy for a lifetime. Such self-centeredness will soon grow old.

A godly person with active faith, who was quick to serve and had the full stamp of approval by God—that was the ideal wife for Isaac. And trust me, that type of person is going to make the best marriage material for any person seeking a mate. A self-centered, lukewarm person without the stamp of God's approval is to be avoided.

PURITY IS GOD'S CHARACTER TEST

How can you evaluate whether someone has good character, possesses an active faith, is virtuous, and has a servant's heart?

When God evaluates a person's character, He looks for evidence of purity. Sin pollutes. Compromise clouds. The English word for "character" comes from the Greek word *cherax* or *cherasso,* each of which refers to the chiseling that is done by a metal engraving tool. Character refers to things that have been etched so deeply into a person's soul that they are lasting marks, not easily changed or removed. Character is manifested in holiness, honesty, morality, temperance, and commitment to the Lord. Look for those traits.

HOW TO DISCERN GOOD CHARACTER

How can you discern good character traits? After all, you can't just walk up to a person who appears to be your kind of person and say, "Hey, do you have good character?" If you do, you're likely to get a line a yard long.

Behavior in Stressful Conditions

The best way I know for you to discern character is to observe what happens to that person when "pressed." Recall that the woman in the Song of Solomon was attracted to his name being like "purified oil." This oil comes from olives that are pressed. When great pressure is applied to ripe olives, out comes pure oil.

What happens to that person for whom you feel attraction when he or she is under pressure or feeling stressed out? What type of behavior does he manifest when things aren't going his way, when times are tough, when deadlines are looming, when cash is in short supply, when he is having a bad day, or when someone hurts or rejects him?

Does the person manifest anger, withdraw to sulk in resentment, have a pity party that goes on and on, speak bitter or unkind words, shout obscenities, or seek revenge? If so, choose to be unattracted to that person as quickly as possible. That behavior is flowing from deep within. Change is certainly possible for such a person, but that change is likely to come slowly over time and be a sovereign work of God. Anger, bitterness, resentment, hatred, sullen and dark moods, and acts of revenge are all traits that I advise you to flee.

"But he's not like that with me," you may say.

"She doesn't do those things in our relationship," you may say.

Trust me. If the person to whom you feel attracted acts this way toward others who disappoint, hurt, or cause him stress, he will eventually manifest that behavior toward you. Maybe not today or tomorrow, or even next week or next month, but eventually.

You may be thinking, *I've watched this person for quite a while and I've never seen her under stress. I don't think she gets stressed.*

Wait longer. Every person feels pressure at some time or other. Negative circumstances or situations totally beyond her control will eventually come around. Wait for that time to come. Observe the person closely when it does.

Reputation with Others

The woman in the Song of Solomon declared, "The virgins love you." He had a solid reputation. He wasn't just good-looking, but he was someone all the young women wanted to date.

What kind of reputation does the person to whom you are attracted have with other Christians, both of the same and of the opposite sex? Does the person have a reputation for obeying God?

The woman told Solomon what she and the other women thought: "We will be glad and rejoice in you. We will remember your love more than wine" (Song 1:4). The women considered it a privilege, a delight, and 100 percent noble and right to be with Solomon!

Ask yourself:

- Would I feel honored to be asked out on a date by this person?
- Would I feel privileged to be seen in church with the person to whom I am attracted?
- Would I love to bring this person home to meet Mom and Dad, Grandpa and Grandma, Aunt and Uncle?

You will be proud to be seen with and proud to have dated a person who has genuine character *even if the two of you break up and the dating doesn't lead to courtship or marriage.*

I meet many young people who say, "Oh, I'm just dating this girl. She's not the type I'd marry. This isn't serious. It's just for fun."

My question is this: "Why *aren't* you dating the type of person you would marry? What is keeping you from doing that? Are you aware that if you date the type of person you wouldn't marry, you are creating your own reputation so that the type of person you would marry may not give you a second look?" You should always be in a position to say, "I am proud to have been seen with, to have dated, or to have courted that person in my past."

Obedient to Authority

The desire and attraction that you feel for another person should have this element: the person is obedient to authority. Each of us is under some type of authority—for example, children are under the authority of their parents, parents are under the authority of pastors and various civic authorities. God has a chain of command in effect, and we are required to be obedient to those in authority as unto the Lord. Much has been said in our world today against submission, but submission is a theme running throughout the Bible. Each of us is required to submit to someone, at some time, regarding some thing.

The woman in the Song of Solomon began to lament her situation:

> *I am dark, but lovely,*
> *O daughters of Jerusalem,*
> *Like the tents of Kedar,*
> *Like the curtains of Solomon.*
> *Do not look upon me, because I am dark,*
> *Because the sun has tanned me.* (Song 1:5–6)

The woman believed she was lovely—she didn't have an esteem problem about her physical features—but she did have a problem with the impression she believed she made. Her skin was very dark. The tents of Kedar, a Bedouin tribe, were made of black wool. The curtains of Solomon's palace were a deep purple. The woman was of a sunburned complexion—dark and somewhat ruddy.

Women in that day prized fairness of skin because it meant they were "indoor girls." They hadn't been out in the fields working at hard physical labor; they had been pampered and sheltered inside their homes.

The woman gave the reason for her skin being dark: "My mother's sons were angry with me; they made me the keeper of the vineyards, but my own vineyard I have not kept" (Song 1:6). She hadn't been able to take the best care of her skin—

her vineyard was her physical body—because she had been out working in her brothers' fields. She was obedient to authority. She was a hard worker, not slovenly, lax, or rebellious against the work required of her.

We have other examples of hardworking women in the Scriptures. Consider Ruth the gleaner, Rachel the shepherdess, Zipporah the shepherdess, and the woman in Proverbs 31 who "strengthens her arms." I tell young men routinely, "Marry a girl with some grit in her!"

Are you attracted to a person who is hardworking and obedient to authority? Choose to be! If you are physically attracted to someone who is rebellious against his or her parents—who refuses to submit to or respect parents as well as other authority figures—rethink your attraction. A person who refuses to obey human authority figures is going to rebel against the authority of God. Such a person is not going to want to fulfill the God-given roles required within marriage—a wife to submit to the decision-making authority of her husband, a husband to submit to the decision-making authority of Christ Jesus. Choose instead a person who yields to authority and who not only has respect for God's power and commandments, but also is obedient to God's leading and to keeping God's rules for right living. Submission will be nothing new for the woman in the Song of Solomon.

WHEN ARE YOU READY TO MARRY?

Dating is a prelude to marriage. So many young people are concerned about when they are ready to date. They are ready to date when they are ready to begin the process of choosing someone to marry or when they have convictions they will not compromise.

I have counseled fifty-year-old people, grandparents

even, who were not yet ready to date because they truly weren't mature enough as individuals to marry. They had married and raised children, but in their hearts, they still were not ready for marriage. Until you are ready to begin the process of choosing a mate, you'll find it better not to date one person exclusively. Go out with groups of friends. Make acquaintances and forge friendships. But date when you are ready to marry.

There are several prerequisites for knowing when to begin dating a person to whom you are attracted.

You are ready to date and marry when you have a silhouette in your mind of the kind of guy or girl you will choose to marry, and when you have resolved in your heart that you will not settle for less. I'm not talking about this as a silhouette: "What I really want is a guy who is six-two, with wavy blond hair and green eyes and a great body, makes a hundred thousand dollars a month, and drives a Porsche." God may have such a person for you, but that should not be your silhouette. The problem is that you've given the details of an ideal mate without any outline of character.

A better silhouette would be: "He must love the Lord with all his heart, actively desire to follow God in all things, have a servant's heart, and be the one for me that God chooses. He must be honest, moral, steadfast, and temperate. He must love me as much as he loves himself. He must have a good reputation, handle himself in a godly manner—even in times of stress—and be willing to yield to authority." That's a silhouette with well-defined edges. The details are ones you must trust God to fill in according to His desire.

I heard a young man say about his wife, "She doesn't look at all like the type of girl I thought I wanted to marry when I was sixteen. I had a five-foot-two, eyes-of-blue, cheerleader type in mind when I was a teenager. A shorter, blonder version of a supermodel would have been just fine! My wife, however, is five-eight, brunette, and wouldn't be chosen as the cover girl for a magazine. And now, after five years of marriage to this wonderful woman, I can't imagine being married to anybody else. She is exactly my type." He had defined the right silhouette of character and spiritual traits that he wanted in a spouse, and he had refused to settle for anything less. God gave him precisely the right woman for him.

You are ready to date and marry when you do not have to compromise any aspect of your relationship with God in order to be with the person to whom you are attracted. In the Song of Solomon we read,

> *Tell me, O you whom I love,*
> *Where you feed your flock,*
> *Where you make it rest at noon.*
> *For why should I be as one who veils herself*
> *By the flocks of your companions?* (Song 1:7)

In the time of Solomon, a veiled woman who would appear in midday was a prostitute. The woman stated that she would not practice the immorality of being a veiled prostitute. She would not sacrifice her integrity and her reputation, or her chastity, to get a man. She had convictions.

If at any time you feel that you can't, shouldn't, or wouldn't do something that you know is right before God for you to do, solely for the sake of winning the attention or heart of another person, put on the brakes! If a person laughs at you for praying, discounts the Scriptures and ridicules you for reading your Bible and believing in the truth of the Bible, scoffs at your attending church, or belittles the value of Christian fellowship, take that as a warning. The right person for you as a Christian believer is a spouse who will encourage you to grow in your faith and who will stand strongly by your side in your pursuit of all that God has for you and in obedience of all that God requires of you.

You are ready to date and marry when you are willing to be single rather than to make a bad choice of a marriage partner. For many young people, a point of desperation seems to come when they feel they just have to have somebody. They fear they are going to be left on the shelf, and rather than wait for God's perfect timing and person, they rush out in haste to find the best person who is still available. Many young women who are seniors in college seem to give in to this fear. They want *somebody,* so they are willing to settle for just about *anybody* who pays attention to them and who is willing to get married.

My wife, Teresa, was a member of a sorority at East Texas State. Sorority life may be fine for some young Christian women, but my wife didn't feel it was right for her. She said to herself, "I'm spending too much time looking for a guy." She consecrated herself to God and made a commitment to have only God's best in her life, and she subsequently felt led to attend Texas Women's University, which wasn't coed at the time. She had few dating opportunities. She took the stance, "God, I'll wait on You to bring me the right guy." And indeed, God brought us together.

Until you are truly willing to be single—rather than settle for second best in a spouse—you are not ready to date and marry.

There is more to learn about a person in the dating process, and that's where we go next in the Song of Solomon and also in our progression toward a loving, intimate, and romantic marriage.

You are ready to date and marry when you are becoming the person that your ideal mate is praying about meeting. Remember that a Christian woman is God's daughter. Why would God bestow a man of shallow character on His daughter? Why would He bestow a woman of shallow character on a man who is His son? Make sure that you are becoming an answer to prayer for a seeking Christian person.

Questions to Think About or Discuss

1. *What are the character traits you believe to be the most important to see manifested in a potential mate? Are these qualities different from what you seek in a friend?*

2. *What qualities do you have to offer a potential mate?*

3. *Are you truly willing to be single rather than marry a person who is not a Christian or who is not right for you in God's eyes?*

4. *To what degree do you think it is possible to change another person through your influence and presence?*

5. *What difficulties do you face in moving from tier-one attraction (physical/material) to tier-two attraction (character/spiritual)?*

Two

The Person You Choose to Date

Song of Solomon 1:9–2:7

I was counseling a woman who had gone through a divorce, and she was very distraught as she sat in my office. In the most compassionate voice I have, I said to her, "Sister, lots of people go through a divorce."

"Oh, I'm fine about the divorce," she said. "It's dating again that has me so upset!"

For most of us, dating truly is the best of times and the worst of times. Most of us who have been through the experience can look back and say, "I had my share of disasters." Others sometimes look back—not after they are married, I hope—and say wistfully, "You know, there's one person I wish I could have or would have dated."

In dating, the first and oftentimes major hurdle is getting the person to whom you are attracted to ask you out. Or perhaps more from a guy's point of view, getting up the courage to ask out the girl to whom you are attracted.

I was attracted to my wife long before we began dating. My wife also felt attraction before our first date.

I met my wife when I was a student in Campus Crusade

for Christ in 1973. I noticed a young woman named Teresa Newman, who always seemed to be hauling around a whole gaggle of girls in her Torino. Any time our Campus Crusade director needed something done, he asked Teresa because she was faithful in following through on what she said she would do. She was a pretty girl, but more than that, she was a quality girl. I found myself watching her more and more, and looking for her more and more in a crowd. I began to say to myself, "Now, there's a girl with character. I would want a daughter of mine to be just like that girl. I would want a son of mine to bring home a woman like her."

The more I asked around about Teresa Newman, the more I got a consensus of opinion that she had a good reputation and a good heart.

I started to gather firewood.

Let me explain. If you want to start a lasting fire, you're going to need some kindling and lighter fluid and serious firewood. If you have only the kindling and lighter fluid—which I liken to physical attraction and sexual passion—then you can produce a roaring blaze. The fire will go out in a matter of seconds or minutes, however. To build a really good fire, you need some serious firewood to place on top of that kindling and lighter fluid. You need to put lots of issues related to character and spiritual depth into proper position and context as you date. The glowing coals of love, morality, holiness, devotion, honesty, forgiveness, communication, and love for God take time to develop, and they come from the firewood you gather in the course of discovering more about each other's character and spiritual relationship with God.

How did I gather firewood? I positioned myself a little closer to this young woman during times of small-group sharing. I asked her roommates about her. I went places that I thought she might go, and I accepted invitations to events and social gatherings where I thought she might be, so I could observe her in the ways she responded to others and to various situations.

The flame was ignited one autumn afternoon.

Teresa and I were playing touch football on the same team one afternoon at McKenna Park in Denton, Texas, when she fell and twisted her ankle. I ran over to see if she needed help. I helped her to her feet and then helped her hobble over to the sideline. Her eyes puddled up with tears. I could tell she was in pain.

She sat on the sideline while we finished the game, and then I went back over to her to ask, "How's that ankle feeling, Teresa?"

"Oh, pretty good," she said.

"Would you like for me to drive you home?" I asked.

A fellow I knew was interested in her came up about that time and also asked, "Teresa, can I give you a ride home?" She looked right at him with a degree of coldness in her voice and said, "No. I already have a ride."

And so she did. I took her home. She prepared some hot chocolate, and we talked for about two hours. I thought I had known what a neat person she was before that time, but during that conversation I really discovered how special a woman she was (and she still is). If I had never been allowed to spend another hour with Teresa Newman, I would have concluded after that one afternoon, "Teresa Newman is a marvelous person."

As it turned out, that first one-to-one encounter was more than twenty years and two children ago. She has become only sweeter and sweeter to me. Something clicked that day that allowed us to begin dating. We crossed the invisible hurdle between attraction and dating. We were ready not only to know more about each other, but also to know each other. You can gain a great deal of objective information about a person to whom you feel an attraction, but dating is the time when you gain firsthand knowledge about a person through your conversations and shared experiences. You really learn how a person responds to various situations and what she holds as her innermost beliefs, goals, dreams, and desires.

I don't know what will happen in your particular case to move your feelings of attraction for a person into a dating relationship, but I believe that if you are truly seeking God's best plan for your life, He will unfold the opportunity for dating to you. You'll find a way across that attraction hurdle and into dating.

THREE THINGS REQUIRED FOR SUCCESSFUL DATING

If you are going to be successful at dating, you are going to need these three things:

1. Time

Dating requires that you spend time together to get to know the person—brief, frequent encounters over a prolonged period. Avoid concentrations of time, such as entire days spent together, when you first begin dating. You need time between encounters to process the information you gain about a person. Too much, too soon, and you are likely to leap to conclusions that you would never make if you took the time to remain more objective. Dating requires time for having long, meandering conversations and for participating in public activities together, and in the process, getting to know each other better in a wide variety of settings and circumstances.

Don't hurry the process. The more time you spend dating a person, the better you are going to know the person and the more likely you will be to make a rational decision about whether this is a person you want to marry. Dating is a time of evaluation.

Spend enough time together to see each other in group interaction and in stressful, even crisis, situations. Before any commitments are made, spend time together in the presence of both families, and spend time together doing real-life daily chores. *I am not advocating that you live together prior to marriage*—quite the contrary—but spend time together cooking in a kitchen, doing laundry at a Laundromat, shopping for groceries, running errands, and so forth. You can learn a great deal about a person's values, ability to manage time and money, and personal preferences in such activities.

I know a number of couples who met in college when both partners were living in dormitories. They ate meals together in the college cafeteria, they studied together in the library, and some even attended chapel together at their Christian college. On the basis that they had dated for several months and had spent lots of hours together, they decided to get married. Unfortunately they had never been in each other's home or hometown (except, perhaps, for very brief weekend or vacation visits). Neither had ever lived on his or her own—having to juggle a time schedule that included many mundane chores not in the dormitory routine. Neither had ever handled a budget, been responsible for rent or car insurance, or been responsible for life's basic chores, such as shopping for groceries, preparing meals, or changing the oil in the car.

What a rude awakening they had after marriage! So many of the circumstances and situations that arose after the wedding would have been much easier to handle had each partner first learned to deal with some of life's responsibilities as a single person.

2. A "No Strings Attached" Policy

Dating should not be obligatory in any sense of the word. If you begin to date a person exclusively, you have moved into courtship.

How can you maintain a "no strings" attachment too soon in the relationship? I recommend two things. First, go on group dates. Double- and triple-date with friends who are Christians. You'll gain valuable information about how your date responds to you, how your date responds to other people, and how your date evaluates the behavior of others. Second, stay in public places.

One young man told me, "We went out to the park at night, got in the backseat of my car, and got tempted." He seemed surprised by the fact! What did he expect? If you don't want any strings attached to your dating relationship, avoid putting yourself in a situation for lust to take over. The apostle Paul wrote to the Romans: "Make no provision for the flesh, to fulfill its lusts" (Rom. 13:14).

Francis of Assisi referred to his body as "brother ass" because he felt that his body had a mind of its own and wouldn't do what he wanted it to do. We all know that feeling.

The couple in the Song of Solomon had a picnic out in the open, in full view of the public: "Our bed is green. The beams of our houses are cedar, and our rafters of fir" (Song 1:16–17).

"Bed," in this meaning, refers to a couch that was used for sitting on and sleeping on. They were outdoors, with the cedars and fir trees forming a canopy above them. It was a romantic setting, to be sure, but it was not a private setting.

The woman said, "I feel as if we own the whole world." She felt like a queen with the best-ever mansion, yet there was no illicit relationship, no sexual encounter. Her feelings were of great freedom because there were no strings attached to their relationship, no cloudy issues, no unresolved gray areas. She knew where she stood with the man and he with her, and at the present stage of their relationship, they were living in individual freedom, yet enjoying each other's company. That's the ideal emotional environment for dating.

3. Respect

A third hallmark of any dating relationship should be respect. Respect and romance are first cousins. A woman who feels that a man respects her automatically feels that a man is being more romantic toward her. Men, if you really want to win the affection of a woman you are dating, show her respect. Express to her how much you like being with her. That's far more important than telling her how much you love her, which may sound insincere to her if you proclaim your love too soon in the relationship.

Have you seen the old Jimmy Stewart movie in which a young man asks the Stewart character for the hand of his daughter in marriage? He says, "Can I marry your daughter?" and Jimmy Stewart replies, "Do you like her?"

The young man responds, "Yes, sir, I love her."

"No," the Stewart character replies, "I didn't want to know that. I asked, 'Do you *like* her?'"

Like is a critical prerequisite to love. If you don't show respect to a woman, she will never believe that you truly like and admire her. And if she doesn't have a sense that you like her, she will find it difficult to believe that you truly love her.

One of the major statements that Solomon made to the young woman was this: "I have compared you, my love, to my filly among Pharaoh's chariots" (Song 1:9). That may not sound like the most romantic line you've ever heard, but let me explain what he meant. The pharaohs always had white horses. A white horse was readily visible for miles. Thus, great homage could be prepared for the pharaoh in advance of his arrival on the scene. The white horse of pharaoh was considered to be a virtual deity, and the horses were considered valuable possessions of the pharaoh. White horses were reserved exclusively for the pharaohs.

Solomon was expressing to the young woman that he saw her as extremely valuable, one in a million! She was beyond any monetary value or comparison.

When you truly respect a person you are dating, you should have this same feeling: you consider the person to be of extremely high value. The person you date should build you up.

So often, young people begin to take for granted the person they are dating. When that happens, the romance fizzles. The same is true for married couples. A woman said to me during a marriage counseling session, "I don't ask that my husband be romantic. I just want him to be civil to me." She went on to say something I'll never forget. She said, "I wish he would treat me like a Denny's waitress."

I thought she was kidding. She wasn't. She explained, "He treats a Denny's waitress with kindness, even saying 'please' and 'thank you.' I never get that kindness."

Kindness is a mark of respect. Respect is necessary for romance. A relationship without romance is flat, even dead.

How did the woman feel about Solomon? She confessed,

> *While the king is at his table,*
> *My spikenard sends forth its fragrance.*
> *A bundle of myrrh is my beloved to me,*
> *That lies all night between my breasts.*
> *My beloved is to me a cluster of henna blooms*
> *In the vineyards of En Gedi.* (Song 1:12–14)

One of the most precious possessions of any woman in Solomon's time was a little pouch of perfumed spices and resins that she wore as a necklace. The pouch gave the woman her scent, which was a significant part of her identity. Have you ever caught the scent of a certain cologne and thought, *That smells like my girlfriend*? Aroma is a powerful identity creator.

And myrrh was one of the most expensive, most potent, and most aromatic resins. The woman was saying, "At night, my thoughts of you are like the aroma from my perfume pouch, which lies between my breasts. Your image fills my mind. I can feel your presence with me. I dream about you."

Let me assure you, a woman doesn't have pleasant dreams about a man who is unkind to her or who doesn't show her respect.

The Combined Whole

Time, a "no strings" policy, and respect—these things ideally blend together during dating. The more time you spend dating a person, the greater your respect should grow. A "no strings attached" policy leads to respect, and increased respect results in both the man and the woman wanting to spend more time with each other. If you want to spend less and less time with a person you are dating, if respect wanes, or if you begin to feel that "strings" are being tied around you so that you no longer feel free to be yourself, back out of the dating relationship. This is not the right person for you!

DESIRABLE THINGS TO EXPECT DURING DATING

When a dating relationship is in good order, each person can expect several things to happen as an automatic consequence of their spending time together.

A Desire to Listen and a Growing Ease in Communication

If you do not experience a growing depth of communication, your relationship is *not* likely to be one that should result in marriage. Communication is a big part of any ongoing relationship, especially a marriage. A typical man tends to feign listening ability during dating. He hangs on every word and makes all sorts of romantic gestures to capture the heart of the woman he desires.

A man is a hunter and conqueror. He is a trophy seeker. He desires to pursue a woman until he captures her love, then keeps her in a cage to do the cooking and housekeeping and bear children while he is off to new conquests. That isn't a marriage; it's a hunting expedition.

Such a man is likely to give the woman he dates a flower every day, but if the woman becomes his wife, she'll probably not see another flower for years.

A key question a woman should ask during dating is this: Does he really listen to me and seek out my opinion and ideas? Any man can do the romantic thing temporarily. Any man can be on his best behavior for a season. Any man can show good manners, a civil tongue, and tender kindness for a while. A man who truly knows how to listen, however, has the capacity to *continue* to listen.

Most women are pretty good at determining if a man is sincere in his listening. Women tend to be excellent communicators, and they know if someone is just pretending to listen or if the person is truly listening, responding, and asking the right kinds of questions.

One of the greatest things you can ever do as a man is to develop good listening skills—not only for your wife's sake, but also for your own sake. Those who are excellent at listening and good at asking probing questions—for example, "How do you feel about that?" "What do you think about that?" "Why do you hold that opinion?"—tend to be slow to anger and slow to argue. They generally acquire more information about what makes another person think and respond as she does, and as a result, they tend to be more compassionate and patient with the other person. Listening is a universal sign of wisdom.

If you find yourself in an argument, apologize quickly and back away to a neutral position from which to listen again with renewed interest. My advice to men is that they never win an argument. Do so and lose a mate. I personally am 0 for 1,000 in my win-loss record of arguments. I let my wife express herself, then I go off by myself, consider what happened that led to the argument in the first place, and try to determine how I might avoid that situation in the future. I replay the conversation, listening more intently with my "spiritual ears" to what was truly taking place. If there are changes to be made, they are much better discussed in calm and peaceful terms at a time when emotions aren't running high and an argument isn't in full swing. Good listening nearly always results in better understanding and greater peace.

A person who feels as if she is talking to a wall, does not seem to be getting much feedback, or feels totally shut out of a conversation because her opinions and feelings don't matter should take a long, hard look at the dating relationship. If a person doesn't listen intently to you during dating, he isn't likely to listen to you intently after you are married.

The woman had a profound sense that Solomon was paying attention to her and to her alone. She said,

> *I am the rose of Sharon,*
> *And the lily of the valleys.*
> *Like a lily among thorns,*
> *So is my love among the daughters.* (Song 2:1–2)

What a change from her view of herself earlier (Song 1:5)! Solomon had raised her self-esteem. She felt the same about Solomon: “Like an apple tree among the trees of the woods, so is my beloved among the sons” (Song 2:3).

Each phrase is in the singular. Roses and lilies are rare flowers in the Middle East. They bloom quickly and appear only for a brief season. They are beautiful and highly valued. In like manner, apple trees are not frequently cultivated in the Middle East. They are rare and highly prized. An apple tree has fruit that neither a fir nor a cypress tree has. What is the interpretation of these statements? The two people—Solomon and the woman in his song—were totally caught up in each other’s presence. They didn’t see or hear anybody else around them; they were focused completely on each other. They were listening to and intensely interested in each other. They saw each other as one of a kind, one in a million, and they valued the time they spent together.

A Growing Feeling of Endearment

During dating you discover whether you have feelings of endearment for the person you are dating. Do you find yourself wanting to call her by pet names? Do you have a loving nickname for him?

Couples who are deeply in love and have a good marriage usually have terms of endearment reserved exclusively for their spouses. It might be “sweetie,” “doll,” or “darling.” I tend to call my wife “sugar” or “honey.”

When did I first begin to use these terms? As we progressed in our dating relationship and grew in tenderness and appreciation.

If you do not feel protective, comforting, or loving toward the person you are dating, or do not find yourself feeling affection to the point that it overflows into your vocabulary, reconsider your relationship.

Criticism or a belittling attitude can quickly destroy feelings of endearment in a dating relationship.

I was counseling a husband and wife who were having some serious problems in their marriage. I immediately noticed how often the husband interrupted his wife to correct her. Many of his statements about her, including ones he made in her presence, were critical. She did not have the same level of education that he had, and he often referred to her lack of intelligence or her lack of information. At times, his tone was outright mocking.

How had she responded to the growing criticism over the years? She had lost all interest in him sexually. She had closed the bedroom door to him. Frankly I couldn't blame her for her actions. Who wants to give herself to a disrespectful person who demeans her for twenty three and a half hours a day and then expects pure bliss from her the remaining half hour?

Over the years this woman's self-esteem had plummeted to an all-time low. Physically she looked like a model. She was so beautiful that men were often very self-conscious talking to her. Yet she had no understanding of her beauty. She felt ugly and stupid.

In a word, all endearment had vanished from the relationship. A critical tongue killed it.

If the person you are dating dumps a load of criticism on you periodically or completely ignores you in a group—both of which can cause a feeling of inferiority or insignificance—seek to end your dating relationship. The criticism and abandonment will not decrease with marriage; they are much more likely to increase.

Dating is a time for building each other up, for seeking out the best in each other and appreciating these traits. Nothing takes the place of a genuine compliment during dating. Such a positive comment says to the other person, "I recognize the goodness in you."

Let me add one more thing about abusive behavior since a precursor to many cases of physical abuse is verbal abuse. If you experience any abusive behavior whatsoever in your dating relationship—verbal, emotional, physical, or sexual—get out of the relationship as quickly as you can. Abusive behavior does not disappear over time; if anything, it intensifies, and its eruptions have increasingly catastrophic results. Abuse is not rooted in love or hate; it is rooted in issues related to power and self-identity within the abusive person. The issues are not easily resolved, and if you are the date of an abusive person, it is not your role to resolve them. You should feel 100 percent safe in the presence of a person you are dating *at all times.*

The woman felt completely safe in Solomon's presence: "I sat down in his shade with great delight, and his fruit was sweet to my taste" (Song 2:3). She was entirely at ease with Solomon. She experienced no threatening or unsettling moments in his presence. The apostle Paul told us that a man should nourish and cherish his wife. (See Eph. 5:29.) The woman experienced that in their premarital relationship. In his "shade" she was cherished. By his "fruit" she was nourished. And note: this must start *before* marriage. Never trust a future mate to do a turnaround after marriage.

Safety and endearment are nearly always expressed in good manners and acts of kindness. Let me give a few words of advice to men. Never walk in front of the woman you are dating or in front of your wife. Walk by her side. Pull out her chair for her. Open the door for her. Treat her as if she is your singular rose, the most precious person in your life.

Let me also give a few words of advice to women. Never tear down the reputation of the man you are dating, especially in the presence of others. Build him up. Thank him for his kindness to you. Appreciate all he does on your behalf. Treat him as the only apple tree in a pine forest.

A Lack of Pressure

Do you feel any pressure from the person you are dating to do things that you don't believe are right before God? Is the person asking you to go places or to engage in activities in which you are spiritually uncomfortable?

A woman told me this story about her dating experience. She had liked two boys at the same time when she was in high school. The boys were friends, and the three of them often went out together on group dates. She liked some things about one boy, other things about the other boy. She said, "If I had been forced to choose, I'm not sure which choice I would have made—until the night we went to the movie."

She and the two young men had gone to an R-rated movie just shortly after movies were rated. They went more out of curiosity to see what an R-rated movie was like than because they desired to see the particular movie. When certain disturbing scenes came on the big screen, the young woman felt uncomfortable and began to fidget. One of the boys leaned over to her and said, "Just relax, this scene will pass. It'll be all right." The other young man said, "I think we should get up and leave. It isn't right to be seeing this." He stood up, the young woman stood up also, and the two of them left the theater, leaving their third friend behind to watch the rest of the movie.

Which young man do you suppose this woman went on to date and several years later, to marry? Of course, the guy with the courage to say, "No, this is wrong." He was also the guy who was sensitive enough to her feelings to know that even if *he* hadn't initially felt anything was wrong with the movie, he was aware that *she* was uncomfortable and he acted in her best interests.

If you are feeling pressured to engage in acts that you believe are immoral, take note! The person you are dating apparently doesn't fear the standard of God in a dating relationship. And believe me, if he will not obey God when you are dating as single young adults, there is very little likelihood that he will suddenly begin to obey God once you are married. If the person you are dating puts his own "needs" ahead of God's commands, he very likely will continue to be a me-first person in marriage, oblivious to God's call on his life to love you as Christ loves the church.

The couple in the Song of Solomon drew close spiritually, socially, and emotionally, but no physical touch occurred before marriage. The man would in no way cause the woman to compromise her faith.

An Open Acknowledgment of Your Dating Relationship

If you are dating a person, you should not care in the least that the entire world knows it. This is not a time for secrecy or hidden agendas.

I recently heard about a woman who was in her thirties, had never been married, and had dated a young man for two years. She finally broke off their relationship despite her deep feelings for him. Why the breakup? In those two years, he had never once suggested that they go over to his parents' house for a visit, even though they lived only twenty miles away in a neighboring town.

He had told her that he didn't want to upset his parents with the fact that he was dating someone, and that he didn't want them to pry into his life. She came to realize that he didn't care to go public about their relationship. Not only was he reluctant to take her to his parents' house, but he always seemed to prefer to stay at home and watch a video rather than go out to dinner or be seen with her in public places. He told her that he wasn't embarrassed about their relationship, but all of his actions said otherwise. He was hiding something—either her from the world or the world from her.

The woman and man in the Song of Solomon had an open-to-the-public relationship: "He brought me to the banqueting house, and his banner over me was love" (Song 2:4). The banqueting table was a large area, usually occupied by many people. Solomon wasn't at all ashamed to let the entire world know he was dating the young woman.

And that's the way it should be. Not that you engage in a great deal of PDA (public display of affection), but that you are not the least bit ashamed for any person to know that you are dating. If you have any qualms at all about what others will think if they discover you are dating, question your relationship seriously. You should be dating someone who has the full approval of all who truly love you and desire God's best for you.

Notice, too, that the woman stated, "His banner over me was love" (v. 4). A banner was used in many ways in the Scriptures, and nearly all of those ways applied to the romantic relationship developing between Solomon and the woman. A banner was

- *a mark of identity.* A banner was used in war to identify a king's troops. The woman had no doubt as she entered the banqueting hall that she was with Solomon. She knew he had chosen to be identified with her and to have her identified with him.
- *a mark of presence.* Kings who had multiple residences often used banners to indicate when they were at home in a particular palace or fortress. The woman knew when she walked into the banqueting hall that all eyes were upon her and that everybody in the room knew that she was with Solomon and he was with her.

They had arrived as a couple, and they would depart as a couple. They were at home with each other in the midst of that public setting. They were with each other, present to each other. Any person who might intrude into their relationship was only a temporary visitor, not a resident of their relationship.

- *a canopy of spiritual blessing.* Even today in Jewish weddings, a prayer shawl is suspended like a banner above the couple being married. It is a sign that the two are becoming one flesh, one identity, and that what they are doing is acknowledged as good and right before God. They are going to dwell under the same tent and under the blessing of God.

The woman in the Song of Solomon felt a banner of love over her. She had a knowing in her spirit that Solomon was doing the right thing by her before the Lord and that their relationship was in good spiritual order. Nothing had been done to violate the purity or sanctity of their relationship. They were candidates for all of God's blessings.

A PERIOD OF GROWING PASSION

A natural phenomenon of dating is a desire to give of oneself. The more respect a person has for another, and the more time spent together, the more the desire to express respect and affection in tangible, physical ways. A part of this growing desire is certainly a sexual desire.

The first line of intense sexual passion that we find in the Song of Solomon is this: "Sustain me with cakes of raisins, refresh me with apples, for I am lovesick" (Song 2:5).

You may protest, "Tommy Nelson, you have a strange

sense of passion and romance if you think those words relate to sexual arousal." But let's take a look at what those lines meant in Solomon's time. The woman was clearly saying, "I *want* this man. I want to have sex with him."

Why raisin cakes? Raisin cakes were highly regarded love enhancers in Solomon's time.

King David brought the ark of the covenant into Jerusalem with much fanfare and celebration. At the time the ark finally was placed in Jerusalem, the nation was at peace and united both politically and spiritually. There were joy in the land and a growing sense of prosperity. The kingdom had been established, righteousness was prevailing, and the covenant with God (established through Moses) was expected to be enjoyed. It was a time for men in military service to settle down and raise families.

After David had finished making burnt offerings and peace offerings to God in thanksgiving for the safe arrival of the ark, he blessed the people in the name of the Lord. Then he distributed among all the people—both to women and to men—a loaf of bread, a piece of meat, and a cake of raisins, and then he sent each person back to his own home. (See 2 Sam. 6:19.)

A cake of raisins was considered to be an aphrodisiac. The raisins were considered to be "seeds" that could increase the "seed" of a couple so that conception was enhanced. In very broad and general terms, David was sending his soldiers home to have a nice dinner and then share good and productive sex with their wives. Raisin cakes were used also in pagan fertility rituals with the expectation that children would result. (See Hos. 3:1.)

What about apples? "Apple" is our English translation of several types of fruits considered to be of the *pome* order—fruits including quince, apple, pear, and pomegranate. The fruits were rich in color and rich in readily identifiable seeds, especially the pomegranate, which is probably the true "apple" in this verse. Pomegranates were considered to be very sexual—juicy, ripe, seed-filled, rich in red color—all analogous to sexual organs and the fruitfulness of the human body.

The woman truly was lovesick. She had so much passion that she almost felt nauseous. She could hardly wait to have sexual intercourse with Solomon. She ached to be one with him. Consider her next words: "His left hand is under my head, and his right hand embraces me" (Song 2:6).

Her eager anticipation was for sexual intercourse; the statement was a description of a sexual position. She was longing for Solomon to cradle her in his arms and fondle her.

The Need for Restraint

As two people court, moving closer and closer to a decision about marriage, their passion should naturally grow. This is part of God's design, His plan, His purpose.

Some people adopt a posture of such extreme holiness that you wonder how they ever have children. Where do they think sex and passion and desire come from? They are gifts from God, who made us to bear children and knew that passion and desire would be parts of the human sexual experience.

Did you know that for many centuries, Jewish boys were not permitted to read the Song of Solomon because the book was believed to stir strong sexual passion? The book is erotic and intoxicating in its references to sexual love. This first reference is only one of many such references, and it occurs during the period in which we might say the couple were courting. Their love had not yet found fulfillment in marriage, and they had not yet experienced a sexual union. Even so, they were anticipating both marriage and sex.

Let me be very clear about one thing. At no time in God's Word is sex apart from marriage considered honorable, right, or in keeping with God's plan. Marriage first, sex after the vows are said—that is God's plan. Sexual promiscuity, living together before marriage, and sex outside marriage are wrong in God's eyes. No extenuating circumstances. No "ifs." No "ands." And no "but what abouts?" Sex outside the bounds of marriage is labeled in the Scriptures either as fornication (between unmarried participants) or as adultery (one or both participants are married). And the Bible records the negative consequences, some of them quite severe and even deadly, that follow from fornication and adultery.

Is this message of restraint and marriage-only sex in the Song of Solomon? It certainly is, and it appears right after the woman's exclamation of her sexual desire. Solomon asserted,

> *I charge you, O daughters of Jerusalem,*
> *By the gazelles or by the does of the field,*
> *Do not stir up nor awaken love*
> Until it pleases. (Song 2:7, emphasis added)

Two interpretations are possible. First, the gazelle is an antelope—one of the sleekest, most beautiful of all animals, rare in the Middle East but highly valued. It is lean, supple, and youthful in its appearance, easily startled and flushed from its hiding places. The same is true for the doe, a female deer. It is considered a gentle, easily awakened or frightened animal, beautiful and tender in appearance but quick to take flight. Solomon was saying, "I adjure you, young women, do not allow your natural, youthful sexual desires to be quickly inflamed. Do not rush into a sexual encounter like an innocent gazelle is flushed from a thicket. Do not awaken sexual passions before they can be rightfully expressed within the marriage relationship."

Another interpretation is that a gazelle is a beautiful,

gentle creature. A man should treat a woman as such. Consider Proverbs 5:19: "As a loving deer and a graceful doe, let her breasts satisfy you at all times." Solomon could have been expressing, "You are too precious and lovely in my sight to ever harm."

In either case, Solomon was saying, "What this woman feels for me is good—in fact, it's great, it's fantastic. But not yet, Dear. Wait just a little longer." How balanced is this book's treatment of sexuality! It presents sex as truly passionate and good and yet holy and intended for God's ordained moment.

Let me add a little Shakespeare to Solomon. Prospero was speaking to Ferdinand, who asked for the hand of his daughter in marriage:

Prospero:

Then, as my gift and thine own acquisition
Worthily purchased, take my daughter: but
If thou dost break her virgin-knot before
All sanctimonious ceremonies may
With full and holy rite be minister'd,
No sweet aspersion shall the heavens let fall
To make this contact grow: but barren Hate,
Sour-eyed Disdain, and Discord shall bestrew
The union of your bed with weeds so loathly
That you shall hate it both; therefore take heed,
As Hymen's lamps shall light you.

Ferdinand:

As I hope
For quiet days, fair issue [children], and long life,
With such love as 'tis now, the murkiest den,
The most opportune place, the strong'st suggestion

Our worser genius can, shall never melt
Mine honour into lust, to take away
The edge of that day's celebration.

In case you didn't catch the full meaning of this older version of English, Prospero was warning his future son-in-law, "If you violate my daughter before the wedding, God will curse your sex life after your wedding." Ferdinand declared that even the devil (the strong'st suggestion, our worser genius) couldn't make him do that because he really wanted a loving wife, a quiet temperament to his home, children, and a long life.

And in your heart, so do you.

Keep the Fires Contained

Would you set a fire in your living room? No? Do you have a fireplace in your home? If you have a fireplace, you likely set a fire in your living room, but you keep it contained in the device made explicitly for keeping a fire contained—your fireplace made of brick, glass, metal, with pokers and screens all designed to keep the fire precisely where you want it.

That same analogy applies to sexual fire in a relationship. Keep it in bounds. A fire kept in bounds provides warmth, happiness, and comfort. Out of bounds it destroys everything in its path.

As I lay in bed with my wife on our honeymoon, I thought repeatedly, *Sex sure is a neat institution!* I didn't feel as if I had to write a love letter to tell my wife how I felt about her. I could show her my love in a fullness of physical response. At the same time, I realized that had I tried to express to her my feelings by the vehicle of sex prior to our marriage, she would not have perceived that my meaning was love; rather, she would have felt used or, at the minimum, led away from

God's commands. Prior to marriage, we both would have felt guilt, which would have damaged our relationship. After marriage, we both felt tremendous freedom, release, and joy. Sex enhanced our relationship like the frosting on a cake.

Sex outside marriage always follows a law of diminishing returns. Why? Because the emphasis is on sex, and sexual gratification by itself is consuming and escalating. Just as a fire out of bounds grows and grows until it rages out of control and destroys everything in its path, so, too, with sex outside marriage.

Remember the first time you held hands with a person of the opposite sex and it meant something to you? It was like six hundred volts of electricity going into your hand, probably to the point that your palm got a little clammy! The first time you put your arms around someone's waist or held a person tight—more voltage! But once you had moved to holding a person tightly or kissing a person, hand holding was no big deal. The thrill of it had been replaced by a greater thrill. And such is the escalation. I don't care if you are a Texan or an Eskimo or an African, the escalation is nearly always the same: head to head, face to face, mouth to face, mouth to mouth, hand to body, body to body. Eventually a sexually illicit relationship peaks and burns itself out, just like a wildfire that finally rages all the way to a river's edge.

Keeping a fire going requires boundaries and appropriate fuel. In marriage, that fuel is growing respect, tenderness, admiration, mutual desires and dreams, mutual Christlike relationships with others (extended family, children, friends, business associations, community relationships), memories and traditions established over time, romance and ongoing expressions of affection, and so forth. Sex outside marriage does not have either boundaries or appropriate fuel.

Sex is demanding outside marriage. Each person demands

"rights," insisting on gratification of self. Sex within marriage takes on an entirely new dimension, that of giving to the other, including those times when desire may not be strong. A godly man is going to understand and maintain respect for his wife in those times when she is unable or undesirous of ardent sexual encounters. A godly woman is going to understand and maintain respect for the needs of her husband and do her best to satisfy those needs, even at times when she is not feeling particularly amorous. Why is this true in marriage and not in sexual relationships apart from marriage? Because marriage involves a lifelong commitment; the expectations and "giving" motivations associated with a long-range view of a relationship are very different from the expectations and "getting" motivations in a relationship where neither party truly can count on the other person being there in the morning.

Dating is a time for growing restraint. A balance must be struck. Pace yourself. Keep yourselves within boundaries. Choose to live out your relationship according to God's plan rather than according to your hormones. Hormones tend to run amok very easily.

In all situations, a person will choose to live according to God's way or man's way. The problem with man's way is that it changes and always fails. God's plan, on the other hand, is always perfect, directional, prescriptive, and rewarding.

Keeping sexual behavior in the right context in dating is tantamount to this advice (which we will look at again in the next chapter) in the Song of Solomon: "Catch us the foxes, the little foxes that spoil the vines, for our vines have tender grapes" (Song 2:15). Don't let anything sneak in and spoil the purity of your relationship during courtship. You will be shortchanging yourself of many benefits down the road. Your bodies are precious vineyards. Protect them!

THREE QUESTIONS TO ASK WHILE DATING

As you date, look for the spiritual disciplines and spiritual direction evident in the life of the one you are dating. Don't rely on "someday I want to" or "I know I need to" or "after I'm married, I hope to" statements. Look for the evidence *today* in the life of the person you are dating. If you don't find it today, there is little chance it will spontaneously appear tomorrow and last into the next decade. Spiritual disciplines and direction flow naturally from an individual's relationship with the Lord. They should not be things that a person initiates or begins to do simply to enhance a dating relationship. Ask yourself,

1. Does the person have a daily quiet time with the Lord?

Few spiritual disciplines are as revealing as this one. If a person has a daily quiet time with the Lord—to read the Scriptures and communicate with the Lord in prayer—then that person is putting himself into a position to be led and directed by the Lord on a daily basis. His faith is alive and active. His intent is focused. He is disciplined in his walk with the Lord. Nothing gives greater security than knowing of a mate's unwavering devotion to Jesus.

Such a person is someone the Lord can convict and nudge into right behavior very easily—including convicting that person when he treats you improperly and nudging that person into the right ways in which you should be treated before the Lord. A person with a daily discipline of being with the Lord is a person whom the Lord can change and transform. And believe me, it's much better for the Lord to be nagging your beloved spouse into right paths and right behaviors than for you to be in that role.

My wife, Teresa, has missed having a quiet time with the

Lord only one day in the last twenty years. On that day, she had surgery, and the surgeon inadvertently cut an ovarian artery. While she was in the recovery room after the surgery, she began to go into shock, and as she was about to die, they rushed her back into the operating room, repaired the damage, and saved her life. On that particular day, she didn't have a quiet time with the Lord. The next day, however, when she couldn't even focus her eyes, a man from our church visited her, and she asked him to read to her from the Scriptures.

2. Is the person involved actively in a Christian church or other body of believers?

My wife did not go to a couple of Campus Crusade meetings and then drop away when she didn't find somebody to date. She was not a sporadic churchgoer. To the contrary, she was deeply committed to the Christian groups to which she belonged, and she could be counted on to be a faithful member through good times and bad.

3. Does the person desire to pursue the same type of spiritual life and ministry that you desire to pursue?

My wife and I have several wonderful things in common. We both want to win people to Christ. We want to be able to share the gospel with as many people in our lives as possible. My wife has a special heart for leading children to the Lord, and I also have a great love for young people.

I quickly discovered in my dating relationship with Teresa that she was more than willing to be a pastor's wife. She hadn't grown up as a pastor's child, and neither had I, but we both desired to serve the Lord and were willing to make the sacrifices necessary to be in full-time church-related ministry.

If you discover during a dating relationship that the Lord

has a specific call upon the life of the person you are dating, and you can't relate fully, completely, and wholeheartedly to that call, back away from dating further. You may be on a similar path now, but eventually a "Y" is going to appear in the road and you are likely to be going in two different directions that will become increasingly divergent. Find a person who is running in the same direction at the same speed you are. If you continue alongside each other, you just may decide you want to run together!

DEVELOPING AN "US" IDENTITY

As you thumb back through this chapter, I hope you discern that the longer you date a person, the more you should feel as if you are developing something between you that has an "us" identity to it. You should start to feel as if you are a team of two, walking in the same direction, of like mind and heart before the Lord, eager to work together and to pull together at tasks that may become mutually yours. If you do not have a sense of growing together, then you must face up to the fact that you are probably growing apart. Dating will put you into one mode or the other—either moving toward each other or moving away from each other.

Don't fear putting an end to a dating relationship that seems to be going nowhere. Thank God for the good times you have enjoyed together and the lessons you may have learned about yourself and about how to relate to other people. Then move on. Those who force a relationship to endure are likely to be in a relationship that forever requires great effort and affords little mutual satisfaction.

When you find a person you enjoy dating—a person with whom you have increasingly good communication and a growing spiritual kinship, for whom you have continued respect and greater feelings of endearment, and about whom you have no embarrassment and no fear—you will eventually come to the point where you begin to court that person.

Courting is different from mere dating—both for the couple in the Song of Solomon and for us today. The term may sound old-fashioned, but courting is a vital step in a growing relationship marked by love, intimacy, and romance. It's a wonderful season to experience!

Questions to Think About or Discuss

1. *Does your dating relationship have the three hallmarks of time, a "no strings attached" policy, and respect?*

2. *What would cause you to stop dating a person once you started a dating relationship?*

3. *Are you a better person and a better Christian because of your dating relationship?*

4. *What do your strongest Christian friends think about the person you are dating?*

Three

The Wonderful Period of Courtship

Song of Solomon 2:8–3:5

Courtship can be a wonderful season in the developing romantic relationship of any couple. Courtship is also an important period. It is worthy of a couple's utmost consideration.

A bad date can be quickly forgotten. It may cost you a little time, a little money, and perhaps a little annoyance. A bad courtship, however, can cost you a piece of your soul—your emotional and mental substance.

Dating is observation. Courtship is involvement.

Dating is a time allotment; it is an end in itself. Courtship is directional; it is moving toward something.

Dating has no strings attached. Courtship involves some mutual responsibility, more vulnerability, and a greater need for trust.

Dating is marketing. Courtship is negotiating a potential sale to its close.

A person once said to me, "What you are saying is that dating is casual and courtship is serious." I hadn't thought of it in precisely those terms, but she was right. Unfortunately in our society at large most young people take dating very seriously, and then they just continue to date without really taking the idea of courtship seriously. Few people truly have a clear understanding about when they move from dating to courting.

WHAT IS COURTSHIP?

Courtship is the time when you begin to date one person exclusively, frequently, and with the purpose of determining if this is the person with whom you truly want to spend the rest of your life. Courtship begins with a decision to date only one person and ends in a formal engagement or a definitive dissolution of the relationship. In other words, the end of courtship is either an engagement or a breakup. A good courtship can be exhilarating and joyful.

A courtship that is conducted poorly or ends badly can leave a person feeling bitter, angry, frustrated, disappointed, discouraged, and even depressed. Therefore, let's do courtship right! The Song of Solomon gives us useful guidance.

A "GROWTH" EXPERIENCE

Perhaps the appropriate word to describe a good courtship is *growth.* A couple should experience a growing together in closeness, a growing passion, and a growing identity of "us." Courtship is not only allowing, but also cultivating the growth of a relationship.

The word *courtship* comes from the Elizabethan era in which the ladies of the court were wooed and won by knights and lords of the court through a process of frequent visitation, attention, gifts, and compliments. A man generally asked a woman's father for permission to court his daughter, which implied that the man seriously and openly (in view of the full court) desired to pursue the possibility of marriage. In saying yes to a courtship proposal, the father was granting the man permission to visit his daughter, give her gifts, express his fondness to her in the form of compliments, and accompany her formally to social events. The two young people were rarely left alone, but perhaps were allowed to sit on the porch swing and talk, take walks together in the neighborhood, and perhaps even go on buggy rides with an appropriate chaperone. (The automobile, by the way, totally changed the sanctity of dating and courtship. With the introduction of the automobile, a couple could date in a mobile motel.)

In our world today, courtship is likely to be thought of as going steady. Even though the social norms have changed, a good courtship still should be couched in extreme courtesy and respect. It should be marked by sexual purity. Such a courtship inevitably requires a sense of pacing, flexibility, and sensitivity on the part of both the man and the woman.

Before you begin to date a person, you should have carefully evaluated that person's character. Dating gives you further opportunity to get to know the person from the inside out. Courtship is the time for evaluating consistency and for deepening communication.

CONSISTENCY OVER TIME

We've all known couples who were off again, on again, off again, on again in their relationship. If such a couple end up at a marriage ceremony, those who witness the event and have known the couple for a period of time are likely to think, *This is an upswing. A downswing is sure to follow.* They may even be taking bets with their other friends about how long the honeymoon bliss will last; they just may keep the receipt for the wedding gift in anticipation of a return.

I have met and counseled couples who are worn out from their dating highs and lows, and then they have erroneously concluded, "We don't seem to be doing very well in dating. Let's get married." That's like saying, "I can't bench-press seventy pounds, so let's stack three hundred pounds on the bar." Trust me—if you can't get along with a person for a few hours a day, four or five times a week, you surely aren't going to be able to get along with that person seven days a week for the next fifty years!

I have never seen a good marriage come out of a rocky courtship, just as I've never seen a good courtship emerge from a dating relationship that had frequent bouts of breaking up and getting back together again.

There should be an easiness of compatibility in your dating relationship as you move into courtship. There should be a growing easiness in your relationship the longer you court. Don't continue to add layer upon layer of time and commitment to something that does not have a solid foundation.

DEEPER COMMUNICATION

A growing sense of togetherness is likely to be achieved through increased sensitivity, vulnerability, and depth of communication. Courtship is the time for sharing one's deepest desires, hopes, and dreams. This should come about naturally because trust has been established during dating.

Courtship is a time for telling life stories in detail, for exploring life's future in detail, for sharing freely and fully anything and everything that you desire to share.

In the Song of Solomon, the woman described Solomon this way:

The voice of my beloved!
Behold, he comes
Leaping upon the mountains,
Skipping upon the hills.
My beloved is like a gazelle or a young stag.
Behold, he stands behind our wall;
He is looking through the windows,
Gazing through the lattice. (Song 2:8–9)

Solomon was eager to get closer to the woman. He was joyful in his desire to know everything about her. He was looking into the windows of her heart, gazing through the latticework of her soul to discover her innermost thoughts, opinions, feelings, and secrets. He wanted to know all that there was to know about her. And he was calling to her as he came to her. She heard the "voice" of her beloved! He was just as willing to reveal himself to her as he was desirous of having her reveal herself to him.

If you are courting a person and you suddenly realize that you are bored with the life stories or that you have lost interest in listening to the other person's opinions, call it a day for the relationship. If you feel "out of sight, out of mind" about the one you are courting, call it quits. In courtship, time should kindle, not dwindle, a relationship. There should be an increased desire to discover more and more about each other.

Courtship is a time for baring one's soul to another person, including revealing any dark secrets from one's past.

A person who truly loves you should be able to handle the full truth about you. I met a man who fell in love with, courted, and married a young woman who had once been the "pass around" girl in her college. She had been through twenty or more sexual affairs during her college days. By the time she met the man she later married, she had come to her senses, committed her life to the Lord, and was deeply embarrassed about her past. Nevertheless, she confessed her past to her husband. She wanted no secrets between them.

What was his response? He wept openly for the pain and grief she had suffered. He rejoiced that she had come to Christ. His love for her increased because he saw the transformation in her life as both a miracle from God and an act of courage on her part. He became her protector, loving her in a way that gave her a genuine shield against the world.

What a wonderful blessing he was to her! She had the love of a man who knew all about her past and still loved her. In that atmosphere of unconditional love, she blossomed as a person. She became a highly devoted, trustworthy, and adoring wife, eager to do all she could to express her love to the man who cherished her and valued her despite her past sins.

All situations don't turn out as well as this one, of course. I know of instances where the truth was such that the other person in the relationship couldn't handle it. That being the case, it was wise that the couple broke up because the love between them truly was not a godly, unconditional love. It was a love based on the idea, "I will love you as long as you don't embarrass me, misbehave, or hurt me." Conditional love is never a good foundation for a marriage for several reasons: the conditions tend to change over time, no one can fulfill all the conditions another person might set, and self-righteousness tends to develop, which in turn can give rise to all sorts of manipulative, controlling, angry, and rigid behaviors.

Courtship is a time for making yourself vulnerable to the one you are considering as a marriage partner. It is a time for taking the risk to share what may initially frighten, surprise, appall, dishearten, or shock the one you are courting. Even so, sharing at a level of vulnerability is something you must do. In the process, you will discover a great deal about the person you love. One of the foremost things you will discover is how the person responds to situations that frighten, surprise, appall, dishearten, or shock! Such situations are bound to occur after your marriage and have nothing to do with your past but with circumstances and events that may relate to other family members, including your children. I believe it is far better to have a preview of how a person will respond to the dark, tragic, or disturbing aspects of life *before* marriage than to make these discoveries after the wedding vows are said.

"But why do I have to tell?" you may ask. One young woman said to me, "I made a terrible mistake in my teenage years. I had a child and gave it up for adoption to a Christian couple. I know God has forgiven me for that mistake I made, and I have forgiven myself. It's in the past. Why bring it up?"

Because it will eventually come up. No matter how "buried" you believe a past error or sin may be, it will find a way of surfacing at some time in your relationship. And even if it doesn't, you will always wonder, with a certain degree of guilt for keeping it secret, whether it will emerge and how it may come to light. I encouraged this young woman who made this confession to me, "Bring it up now so that he will know you trust him enough to tell him this story. And be sure to include your feelings of remorse and forgiveness as part of the story. The story you have in your past is not only a story of sin, but also a story of a repentant heart and of forgiveness. Those are vital aspects to any story."

Let Jesus Christ be your role model as you hear and respond to the past life of the person you love: "As Christ also loved the church and gave Himself for her, that He might sanctify and cleanse her with the washing of water by the word, that He might present her to Himself a glorious church, not having spot or wrinkle or any such thing, but that she should be holy and without blemish" (Eph. 5:25–27).

Paul was a zealous persecutor of Christians before he came to Christ, yet God used him mightily. David was an adulterer and murderer, yet God entered into an everlasting covenant with him. Mary Magdalene was a prostitute who was delivered from seven demons, yet Jesus chose to reveal Himself to her first after the Resurrection. Matthew was a despised tax collector, yet Jesus selected him as one of His twelve disciples. Choose to forgive. And allow yourself to experience the forgiveness of unconditional love from the person you are courting. If forgiveness and unconditional love are not flowing freely in your relationship, then Christ is not central to your relationship. Face that fact with forthrightness. If Christ is not central to your relationship, you are on shaky ground, indeed.

Future Hopes and Dreams

Not only must you share fully the events of your past with your possible future spouse, but you must also share your heartfelt dreams and desires for the future. Can you imagine the shock one young woman felt when after two years of marriage, her husband suddenly announced that they were going to Bible school and then to South America to serve as missionaries?

"What happened?" she asked. "Did God speak to you at church last Sunday?"

"No," he said. "I have known since I was fifteen years old that this is what I am supposed to do with my life. I just haven't been in obedience to God."

At the time the young man sought to get back into obedience, he and his wife had been out of college for three years, she was enjoying a very successful track record at the bank where she worked, and he had just been offered a partnership in a young and growing accounting firm. They were expecting their first child and had just made a down payment on a house. She told me that when he shared with her how God had dealt with him as a teenager, a phrase from an old song came to her mind, and her response to him, with a little alteration of the lyrics, was, "You picked a fine time to tell me, Lucille."

He admitted that he hadn't told her about this call of God on his life because he was afraid he would lose her. In his heart of hearts, he had believed that if she married him and was deeply in love with him, she'd go with him anywhere. In the end, she did go with him to Bible school and to South America—willingly, not begrudgingly—but it wasn't because he had kept this dream a secret. It was because God sovereignly spoke to her heart, because she was a woman of great character, and because her love for her husband was unconditional. The couple also went through several difficult months of counseling during which time they both learned how to communicate at a deeper level. To a certain extent, the woman had to overcome feelings of betrayal that she had been enticed into a marriage without a full revelation of her husband's intentions. I applaud her for trusting God and sticking with her marriage vows. I know many women who might have said to this young man very quickly, "Send me a postcard when you get to your destination point. I'm staying here."

Certainly not all dreams or goals are so dramatic, but even more routine dreams—about the house you want to have in the country, the number of children you desire to have, the way you desire to serve God in your community—should be shared during courtship. They should not be idealized images that you share with each other because you think they are the "right" dreams for a Christian young person to have; they should be genuine dreams that you have had for a significant period of time.

Expectations

You should also share your expectations regarding a spouse. I recently heard a story about a young man who married a woman expecting that she would cook dinner every night, keep a neat house, and manage the family checkbook. The young man's mother had done those three things, and she was his only image as to how a wife functioned outside the bedroom. During his courtship days, his girlfriend had cooked a couple of meals for him. She was living at home, and her mother kept a clean, neat home. He automatically assumed that she would do the same. Not once did they have a discussion about how the two of them might divide the various daily-living chores and responsibilities they would face as a couple.

What were her expectations? She hated to cook. She expected her husband to bring home enough money so that they could go out to eat every night or order in meals. If not, she expected *him* to cook. Furthermore, she expected to have a full-time housekeeper. She did not at all want to live the kind of life her mother had lived. She announced to her husband-to-be that she had a deep desire to shop and be a mother, preferably in that order. And to top it all off, she had never had a checkbook of her own and didn't have the foggiest idea how to manage money, make a budget, or balance a checking account.

You can imagine the difficulties the two had in their first few years of marriage as both learned to make serious adjustments in their expectations of what a good wife or husband should do. They had a real struggle in finding common ground on which to build a daily living pattern that was satisfying to both of them.

Don't make promises about how you will live and act after you are married unless you have strong evidence that you have lived and acted in that way in the past. Don't agree to take on responsibilities for things you would like to be able to do but you have never done successfully over time.

True to Yourself

A good courtship should bring out the best in you and allow you to express yourself fully without any feelings of recrimination or apology. You should feel free to be who God created you to be. You cannot endure a lifetime of impersonating your mate's ideal.

I am primarily a people person. I enjoy being with people and working with people. I am not at all handy when it comes to fixing a leaky faucet. I'd rather call a plumber and have a good conversation with him while *he* does the hands-on work.

Fortunately I rarely have to call a plumber because my wife is good at home repairs. Some men buy their wives flowers to make them happy; I buy my wife the tools and appliances she desires. She recently remodeled our kitchen, and I mean that quite literally. She worked right alongside the carpenters and electricians, knocking out walls, removing plaster, painting, installing new lighting, wallpapering, and so forth.

Each of us is true to unique gifts. And that's the way it should be. Courtship is a time for revealing your giftedness to another person and accommodating the other person's gifts. If your giftedness blends together, what a blessing! If your giftedness competes or conflicts, you have a problem.

I heard about a man who had difficulty admitting to his prospective wife that he couldn't drive at night on the freeways where they lived. He suffered from what we often call night blindness. That was a difficult admission to make since a guy generally likes to be the one driving the car on a date across town. His girlfriend at the time, later his wife, had absolutely no problem with his not being able to drive at night. She was delighted to take on that role. His admission gave her the courage to tell him something that she had felt awkward in expressing: she suffered from dyslexia. She knew that her boyfriend's mother did wonderful handwork—needlepoint, embroidery, cross-stitch—and she feared that her husband would expect her to do the same. She found that kind of handwork nearly impossible to do. In making her admission, to her relief, she discovered that her husband didn't care at all whether she did any handwork. He had found the numerous hand-stitched items in his childhood home to be a bit fussy and bothersome.

What a relief to each couple to discover that they could fully be free to be themselves, in strengths and in weaknesses. An admission of one's foibles, flaws, and past sins is almost like a vaccination—it keeps your beloved from being surprised if those aspects of your personality and history crop up later.

If the one you are courting is resentful of your abilities and talents, jealous of your skills or achievements, uptight about your weaknesses or lack of ability in an area, take note. The two of you may have much in common and respect each other, but you may not "fit" together well for the long haul of a marriage.

Honesty and Transparency

Communication at all levels—about the past, present, and future—should become completely honest and transparent in courtship. Such communication is risky, but it is vital to the establishment of a sound marriage. Secrets, facades, and future fantasies can be devastating to a relationship.

"But this is a book about romance," you may be saying. "What does this kind of communication have to do with love and intimacy?"

A great deal. If one person in a marriage relationship suddenly feels conned or betrayed in some way, intimacy and romance are going to fly out the window. It is extremely difficult to be sexually intimate or emotionally vulnerable with someone who is under a load of guilt or fear, or who is highly secretive about the past. It is very difficult to be vulnerable in romance with someone who refuses to open up and share who he is and what he dreams, desires, or hopes—or even worse, with someone who cannot forgive.

Past secrets, untold dreams, and false expectations can cause a person to become "me" focused rather than "other" focused. A self-absorbed person will not be a willing giver of self. This will definitely have repercussions not only in the bedroom but in all areas of a marriage.

Too Much, Too Soon

As important as it is for the two of you to communicate at deep levels and reach a decision about commitment, it is very dangerous to share too much with a person too soon in a relationship. What you share should be at the level of trust you have established between you, and trust takes time to build.

When I was eighteen, I went to a high school dance, and during one particular slow dance, the girl I was with began to kiss me on the neck. I had never been kissed on the neck during a dance before, and even though she only kissed me two or three times, I began fantasizing about what we would name our children! After the dance, we went walking in a nearby park, and she put her arm around me. I was as close to heaven as I had ever been.

The next Monday at school she was very casual when she saw me and said, "Hi ya, Tom." She treated me like every other guy. The Saturday night dance and walk in the park had meant nothing to her, although they had meant just about everything to me that weekend. I had fallen too hard, too fast in my emotional response. She had acted too fast, too ardently at the dance. In all, it was too much, too soon.

Some people are quick to tell you their life stories the first fifteen minutes you know them. Too much, too soon.

Some people are quick to say, "I love you," when they barely know if they like the person to whom they are speaking. Too much, too soon.

Some people are quick to make lifelong plans after a four-hour date, two hours of which were spent watching a movie. Too much, too soon.

Two verses in Proverbs—also ascribed to Solomon, by the way—speak to this very issue:

> *Have you found honey?*
> *Eat only as much as you need,*
> *Lest you be filled with it and vomit.* (Prov. 25:16)
>
> *Seldom set foot in your neighbor's house,*
> *Lest he become weary of you and hate you.* (Prov. 25:17)

Too much, too soon can make you sick of someone!

Courtship is not a time to be rushed. Exploring the depths of another person takes time. So does reaching deep levels of communication. Don't expect a person to become immediately transparent, vulnerable, and totally self-disclosing to you. Neither should you be completely transparent, vulnerable, and totally self-disclosing to others *without first establishing a foundation of trustworthiness, sensitivity, and respect.* Be certain that the person with whom you share your secrets will keep the secrets.

An Ability to Survive Arguments

Can your relationship survive misunderstandings, arguments, and the occasional conflict of interest? If not, take heed.

In the Song of Solomon we find a mutual commitment of the couple to face and resolve difficulties: "Catch us the foxes, the little foxes that spoil the vines, for our vines have tender grapes" (Song 2:15). Foxes are deadly to vineyards because they nibble the early blossoms from the vines. As a result, no fruit will mature from those blossoms. A number of things have the capacity to nip a relationship in the bud before it has time to develop fully. Little foxes might include communication glitches, unthoughtful acts, little resentments and disagreements, colliding differences of opinion, or unchecked premarital passion.

The two of you need to learn to fight clean and to resolve conflicts fairly and in love. Courtship is the time for developing those skills.

One of the most frequent complaints that I hear as a pastor in counseling sessions is this: "I try to talk to my husband, but he won't listen." A woman doesn't need a perfect man, but she does need a man who is perfectible. She needs a man who is willing to listen to her and to take her ideas and opinions into consideration. At the core of many marital arguments is this issue of "you never listen to me; you don't care what I think." Men, if your girlfriend or wife accuses you of poor communication skills, own up to them. In ninety-nine out of a hundred cases, she's right, and the other one case isn't worth fighting about.

A WILLINGNESS TO COMMIT

The humorist Dave Barry once wrote about the reluctance of men to commit to relationships and marriage, "If a man was a chicken breast and you put him in the microwave in July, he wouldn't be ready till Thanksgiving." Men tend to shy away from commitment, very often believing that it will be confining, restrictive, or burdensome. Women are sometimes too eager to jump into a commitment, generally for very different reasons: they are looking for security, support, and faithful love.

Even if you are not yet ready to make a commitment related to marriage, courtship is a time in which some degree of commitment should be expressed openly by both persons in the relationship. Commit to the degree that you are willing and able to commit.

I strongly encourage every young man who is in a dating relationship to say to the young woman after four or five dates, "I don't know if you are the person that God has for me to marry, but I want you to know that you are the type of woman I would enjoy spending my life with, I like being with you, and I'm open to seeing if this relationship goes somewhere. If you want to back out of our dating relationship right now, then that's all right. You owe me nothing but honesty."

If you discover after a few dates that a young woman is *not* the type of person you want to spend your life with, tell her as gently as possible that you don't anticipate that your relationship is going to become a permanent one, and therefore, you think it's probably better that you part ways now rather than later.

Be honest about your feelings and forthright about your intentions. You feel either one way or the other—express your feelings. You'll save yourself and the person you are dating a lot of frustration and heartache. You'll also feel better about yourself for being honest and straightforward.

Mark the point at which you begin to court. Don't just slide into courtship. Make a statement: "We've been dating for a while, and I'd like for us to date each other exclusively. I enjoy your company, and you are the kind of person I'd like to marry. I'd like for us to seriously explore whether we truly are meant to spend the rest of our lives together."

If at any time in your courtship you realize that you are *not* going to marry this young woman, end your courtship as graciously and kindly as you can. Don't muddle along until you both are so hurt, frustrated, and upset that anger and bitterness take root. Above all, young men, do not romance a woman and then in a fit of spirituality decide to be "wholly God's" and leave her. Word will spread about you, and rightly so. Be careful with a woman's heart.

My advice to young women is this: don't press for commitment, but do press for communication. You can say to a man who has dated you several times but hasn't said how he feels about you or your relationship, "I'm not asking for any form of commitment, but I would like for you to communicate to me your feelings. Do you like being with me? Am I the kind of person you would consider spending the rest of your life with? Do you think there's any possibility for this relationship to move to deeper levels?" Although you aren't in a position to either expect or demand commitment, you can certainly probe for information. If the man is totally unwilling to express his feelings, you have your answer. Either he isn't willing to communicate with you, or he isn't feeling anything—both of which mean he is not emotionally involved in the relationship.

The point is, for any relationship to move forward from dating into courtship, and then from courtship to a formal engagement, *somebody* has to do some talking and *somebody* has to initiate the forging of commitment. Men, make that your responsibility. Take the lead!

Parting Ways

If the time comes for you to part ways, do so in a way that leaves the other person encouraged, not devastated. Let the person know that you value the time you have spent together and that you want only the best for the person in the future. Let the person know that you will be praying that God sends him or her the right mate, and then follow through and pray that prayer.

I've been through this. Maple Street Dorm, 1973. A fine Christian girl I had dated for a couple of weeks said to me with sincerity, "I enjoy spending time with you, but I would feel a great peace if God were to take us now in different ways." I wasn't stupid. If she would feel *peace* about God taking me out of her life, then the best place for me to be was out of her life. I was hurt, but I also knew where I stood and where we stood as a couple. I'm grateful now that she made the decision she made and equally grateful that she was able to express her feelings to me in such a kind and positive manner.

A GROWING "US" IDENTITY

During a period of courtship the two people have a growing sense of "us"—of being a unit, an entity, a united front. An "us" identity begins in dating; it grows in courtship.

A man increasingly takes his girlfriend into consideration in making decisions, scheduling activities, making plans, and forming friendships, and vice versa.

Most men have a strong sense of "I." They are used to making decisions solely for and about themselves. Some men find it difficult to develop a "we" perspective. I was one of them.

I grew up in a family with three brothers. Teresa and I have two sons. In my youth, I had a male dog named Johnny. After Teresa and I married, we had two dogs—Roter and Rooter—both obviously males. I truly wasn't used to living with a female creature of any type prior to living with Teresa.

My wife broke me into the idea of a "we" mind-set very quickly. I had one particularly bad habit. If Teresa and I were talking to someone, I had a tendency to move between her and that other person. It was a subconscious act on my part. On reflection, I decided that I was probably trying to define my turf and my domain as a man. Teresa made it very clear, "Tommy, you do *not* do that." I got the message loud and clear. But for months, I had to develop a new pattern of behavior. I had to very consciously, intentionally, and deliberately guard my language and my behavior in order to develop a "we" perspective and attitude. Eventually I did.

Courtship is the time when this mind-set needs to develop. In the Song of Solomon we find this statement:

My beloved spoke, and said to me:
"Rise up, my love, my fair one,
And come away.
For lo, the winter is past,
The rain is over and gone.
The flowers appear on the earth;
The time of singing has come,
And the voice of the turtledove
Is heard in our land.
The fig tree puts forth her green figs,
And the vines with the tender grapes
Give a good smell.
Rise up, my love, my fair one,

And come away!
O my dove, in the clefts of the rock,
In the secret places of the cliff,
Let me see your face,
Let me hear your voice;
For your voice is sweet,
And your face is lovely." (Song 2:10–14)

What a wonderful picture of courtship! Like springtime, their relationship had blossomed fully. Indeed, "love edifies" (1 Cor. 8:1). Solomon was calling to the woman to be with him exclusively. He wanted to be alone with her, and in the "secret places" he wanted to communicate with her, get to know her, and deepen a relationship with her. He was committing to discover all he could about her.

Solomon and the woman eventually reached the point of commitment. She declared, "My beloved is mine, and I am his. He feeds his flock among the lilies" (Song 2:16).

Their courtship brought them to the point of knowing that they were fully meant for each other and that their mutual desire was to be husband and wife. The knowing had come to them in a way that many of us have experienced: we simply no longer want to be apart. We want to be *together,* now and always. Like a lamb led in tenderness to a place of rest, she was totally secure in his love. Read what the woman communicated:

Until the day breaks
And the shadows flee away,
Turn, my beloved,
And be like a gazelle
Or a young stag
Upon the mountains of Bether.
By night on my bed I sought the one I love;

I sought him, but I did not find him.
"I will rise now," I said,
"And go about the city;
In the streets and in the squares
I will seek the one I love."
I sought him, but I did not find him.
The watchmen who go about the city found me;
I said,
"Have you seen the one I love?"
Scarcely had I passed by them,
When I found the one I love.
I held him and would not let him go,
Until I had brought him to the house of my mother,
And into the chamber of her who conceived me.
(Song 2:17–3:4)

Suddenly the clouds lifted; the day broke. She longed for her beloved to return to the "mountains of Bether." The mountains of Bether mean "hills of separation." What are they? They are the breasts of the young woman. (Compare Song 4:5–6 and Song 8:14.) She longed for the one she loved. Night after night she thought and dreamed of him until she sought him out and brought him to her mother, perhaps to hasten the day of approaching marriage. What passion! Do you think that her beloved would condemn her?

Again we find the warning:

I charge you, O daughters of Jerusalem,
By the gazelles or by the does of the field,
Do not stir up nor awaken love
Until it pleases. (Song 3:5)

Passion will grow naturally in courtship. But so must restraint. The Bible treats desire as normal, expected, and good. But there is a divine time and place for it.

Once you have this knowing in your relationship—this awareness that you *are* going to be husband and wife—there is a strong tendency to say, "Well, we're going to be married anyway, let's just go ahead and consummate our relationship sexually."

"No," Solomon said. "Now, more than ever, is the time to choose to wait for sexual fulfillment." Knowing that you are meant to be together before God—and deciding to marry—is one thing. Marriage vows and the consummation of marriage are another.

Courtship ideally results in an engagement to marry. Plans then should move very quickly toward a wedding, in my opinion. I am a strong believer in long dating, long courtship, and a brief engagement. Once the decision is made to marry, it is very difficult to restrain passion. Plan the wedding and get on with the marriage.

Courtship, however, is the time for reaching that wonderful decision. And what joy should fill both hearts. I've found my wife! I've found my husband! Truly this is a time when both a man and a woman should feel as the young woman in the Song of Solomon felt when she said, "I found the one I love. I held him and would not let him go!"

Questions to Think About or Discuss

1. *Does the person you are courting display consistency, a willingness to communicate at deep levels, and a willingness to commit? Why are these elements important to the growth of a relationship?*

2. *How are you handling the growing sexual passion you are feeling toward your beloved during your courtship days?*

3. *In what ways are you developing and manifesting a "we" and "us" perspective?*

4. *Is your courting an easy thing or an up-and-down, make-it-work, forced relationship?*

Four

The Wedding God Desires for You to Have

Song of Solomon 3:6–11

God's plan for any young couple getting married is that they have a holy, pure, and joyful wedding celebration to unite their lives as one spiritually, emotionally, and socially. And then, that they have a glorious, rapturous, and steamy wedding night in which to celebrate their wedding and unite their lives as one sexually.

It's a plain and simple plan. It's also a plan that works.

A recent survey concluded that 80 percent of the relationships in which couples were living together without marriage vows end in separation. Sixty percent of those who are married by a justice of the peace are divorced later. Forty percent of those who are married in churches eventually divorce. And those who read their Bibles together daily divorce only at the rate of 1 out of 1,050!

On that basis alone, and if I had no other reason, I would recommend that a couple wait until marriage for sex, get married in a church as part of a holy and sacramental ceremony, and then read their Bibles together on a daily basis. At the heart of any good marriage is a *spiritual* bond. Sex should flow out of that bond and enhance that bond. But until the spiritual bond is there, fully in place at the time of the wedding, the sexual bond is not likely to hold over time.

As a pastor, when I marry a couple, I stand at the bottom of the steps that lead up to the platform. I greet the people, I thank God for the occasion that has brought us all together, and then I ask both the groom and the bride to make a vow in the name of the Father and of the Son and of the Holy Ghost that they will not divorce each other and will treat each other with kindness, love, tenderness, and sanctity, remaining utterly faithful to each other for the rest of their lives. It is only after they have made such a vow, with a full awareness that to take a vow in the name of God and then turn one's back upon it is to break one of God's foremost commandments, that I invite them to step up to the highest area to consecrate their marriage.

The most important part of any wedding ceremony is the intent of both individuals regarding marriage.

If you are thinking, *Well, I want to get married, but if this doesn't work out as I hope it will, I'll bail out;* if you are thinking, *We've come this far and I'm afraid I'll embarrass myself by backing out, even though I have serious questions about whether I can fulfill my marriage vow;* if you are thinking, *I love this woman, and I want to be with her as long as our love lasts;* or if you are thinking, *I'm not sure whether a person can be faithful to another person* all *his or her life, but I'll be faithful as long as I can be,* you are not ready to marry. You are desiring a sexual affair, not a marriage.

Marriage should be entered into only if you are 100 percent desirous of making a vow before God to love the person who is standing by your side regardless of what happens and for as long as you both live.

A GREAT WEDDING IS A DIVINE APPOINTMENT

A great wedding has several hallmarks. The first is this: a wedding is a holy and divine moment.

Look at the description in the Song of Solomon as this couple entered into marriage: "Who is this coming out of the wilderness like pillars of smoke . . . ?" (Song 3:6). This is a reference to the wandering of the children of Israel in the wilderness, led from place to place by the Spirit of God who manifested Himself in the form of a pillar of cloud by day and a pillar of fire by night.

The couple had a keen understanding that God brought them to that point. Their wedding was a holy moment, a divine appointment. They openly recognized that God was the "author" of their relationship, and they put themselves into a publicly acclaimed position of trusting God to be the "completer" or the finisher of their relationship in the years ahead.

If you are thinking of your wedding as only a legal transition from being unmarried to being married, or as only a party in which you share your love with your friends, think again. Your wedding is a moment both partners should anticipate as a sacred moment. The word *sacrament* means literally "sacred moment," and the sacrament of marriage is just that, the sacred moment of marriage. It is a moment in which God is fully present as the foremost witness to the wedding vows.

A GREAT WEDDING IS A TIME FOR CELEBRATION AND JOY

As Solomon approached his wedding, we have this description of him: "Perfumed with myrrh and frankincense, with all the merchant's fragrant powders" (Song 3:6). Those were symbols of sweetness and celebration. The very atmosphere of the wedding was going to be the very best of the best.

One of the best weddings I have ever seen was one in which I participated at First Baptist Church in Dallas a number of years ago. The groom was a leader of the Hispanic community in greater Dallas and a member of our church in Denton. He married a lovely woman who was also Hispanic. Everything about their wedding had a decidedly Hispanic flair. After another pastor and I had walked to the front of the church, trumpets began blaring at the back of the church. People entered carrying Christian banners, which they brought forward to the front. Then came the dancing girls—yes, dancing girls, right there in the sanctuary at First Baptist—floating and twirling in joyful praise all the way to the front of the church. Then came the bridesmaids and groomsmen, all of whom looked radiant and joyful. Then the bride and her father walked down the aisle in great fanfare. With the entire congregation on its feet, the father declared, "All things have been done in order, this man has courted and loved and done honorably by my daughter." Then he cried to the back of the sanctuary, "Receive your wife!" The back doors swung open, and the joyful groom nearly ran up the aisle to stand before me with his beloved. What a day! What a celebration!

Your wedding may not have that particular flair to it, but it certainly should be a time of joy, sweetness, and happiness. The atmosphere should be filled with laughter, praise, and song. The emotional climate of the room should be warm, with a feeling that no matter what might happen in the way of glitches in the pomp and circumstance, nothing truly matters except the love and happiness of the couple being united in marriage.

Go into your wedding with a glad heart. Celebrate the

fact that God has brought you together, all the way through dating and courtship and engagement to the marriage altar.

A GREAT WEDDING SHOULD HAVE A SUPPORTIVE ATMOSPHERE

Solomon did not go to his wedding alone—far from it:

> *Behold, it is Solomon's couch,*
> *With sixty valiant men around it,*
> *Of the valiant of Israel.*
> *They all hold swords,*
> *Being expert in war.*
> *Every man has his sword on his thigh*
> *Because of fear in the night.* (Song 3:7–8)

Can you imagine how a young woman would feel as she came up the aisle at a wedding ceremony to find that her husband-to-be had sixty groomsmen, all fully armed and ready to fend off anybody who tried to disturb the proceedings or harm the bride? She would no doubt feel very safe and secure. She might easily conclude, "Here's a man who truly is going to protect me."

I once performed a wedding in which a man said something that everybody assumes to be part of the wedding vows but that I had never heard said in just this way. He turned to his bride and said, "I will never divorce you. I will never leave you nor forsake you, and you will be safe in my arms." What a tender and loving commitment to make!

Your wedding ceremony should bear a sense of security, safety, protection, and solidarity. It's not a good sign at all if you suspect there are people sitting out in the pews thinking,

This is a shaky deal, or *She really doesn't know what she's in for; she's marrying a real ogre who is going to abuse her in more ways than she can imagine.* Nobody should be thinking, *They're going to need lots of help if they're going to make it.*

Part of the safety and security of the wedding ceremony will be evident in the people who serve as your best man, maid or matron of honor, groomsmen, and bridesmaids. Choose godly people who will support you fully in the vows you make. As a whole, those who witness your marriage should be like a holy hedge of protection around you, keeping you focused toward each other inside the circle of matrimony, and keeping out anybody who might try to destroy your marriage. Don't ask someone to stand up for you who isn't completely committed to you, to your marriage and, in general, to the sanctity and value of marriage. Such a person will not encourage you to work through problems in your marriage; such a person will not do the utmost to help you and your spouse when you need help. And they may embarrass you at rehearsal dinner!

A GREAT WEDDING IS MARKED BY STRENGTH

A key ingredient of a great wedding is a strong groom. Solomon was a man of notable strength:

Of the wood of Lebanon
Solomon the King
Made himself a palanquin:
He made its pillars of silver,
Its support of gold,
Its seat of purple,
Its interior paved with love
By the daughters of Jerusalem. (Song 3:9–10)

Everything about these two verses speaks of strength and of being established. Solomon was "solid." The cedars of Lebanon, the silver and gold, the royal purple, the extensive embroidery lovingly stitched by the women of Jerusalem. The man had built a "carriage" for himself and his bride that was fully finished and furnished.

Every woman I know wants to marry a man who is strong and who has not only character of substance but real material substance to offer her. Women are drawn to strength.

After thirty-eight years of counseling experience, a counselor made an observation about bad marriages in his book *Passive Men, Wild Women.* He wrote that when a woman realizes that the man she has married is not the same man at home as he is at work, she becomes angry and rightfully so. At work, the man may be creative, passionate, zealous, ambitious, and a leader. At home, the same man may become placid, opinionless, a bad listener, vacillating, uncreative, uncommunicative, and humorless. The fact is, if he behaved at work as he behaves at home, he would never be promoted or rewarded. To the contrary, he would probably be fired. And yet many men fit this dual-personality profile. The counselor concluded that the wives of such men do not rebel; they are merely mad.

A woman wants the creative, passionate, zealous, ambitious, and leader traits to be manifested at home to the same degree they are displayed at work. Certainly a man can be more relaxed and at ease in his home, but when it comes to his relationship with his wife, he should display the same sense of vision, enthusiasm, diligence, creativity, and general people skills that he displays at work. No woman wants leftovers. The feminist Gloria Steinem noted, "We women have finally become the men we always wanted to marry." Sad, but true, in many cases. Women are looking for real strength in men—not abuse, not violent tempers, not overt warfare—but inner strength.

A woman is also looking for a man who will display to her that he loves her enough to provide a place for her, both materially and financially. We have an erroneous notion in our society that it's very romantic for a young couple to get married, penniless but passionate, and then live on love a while. That state of being gets old very quickly. It takes money to have even a modest honeymoon, to set up a home, to provide for another person in your life and, eventually, to provide for children you may have. The income for a family is the husband's responsibility. Many women work these days, but the primary responsibility for earning the money required by a family still rests with the man. And too few men are stepping up to the plate and accepting this primary responsibility.

I've met too many young men lately who expect their wives either to earn at least half of the family income or to support them fully after they are married. My advice to them is to wait. Most women feel a built-in resentment if they are called to support their husbands over a prolonged period of time.

Helping with financial support for a short period of time may be appropriate—for example, if a man works a semester to allow his wife to finish college and then she works full-time for a semester to enable him to finish college. At times, a woman may need to work because her husband becomes ill or injured. As a general rule, however, it is far better to wait to marry until the man can support his wife and family.

When should this decision be made? Not three months before the wedding! This decision should be made as a person starts to court. Then the man and woman can pace themselves through courtship and the engagement period so that they set and reach certain financial and material goals at the same time as they enter marriage.

I heard about a couple who have been happily married

for nearly twenty years. They grew up next door to each other and were childhood sweethearts. They began to date as seniors in high school and on into the first year of college. They then had a three-year courtship in college, followed by a three-month engagement. Early in his life, this man made four promises to himself: he would marry when he had finished college, had a job, was able to give his future bride a diamond ring that he would be proud for her to wear, and had saved ten thousand dollars.

What did his girlfriend, later wife, think about this? She was thrilled! Each promise reflected to her that he had focus, determination, and a desire to give her his very best.

Young man, if you have been spending all of your earnings on yourself, without any regard to your girlfriend and your future together, you aren't ready for marriage. What do you have to offer this woman that will give her comfort and a feeling of value and security?

"Well," you may say, "I'm giving her myself!"

True enough, but what else? What outward and tangible signs can you offer that you will not draw her into a life of debt, waste, meagerness, stinginess, and constant worry about finances? What plans have you made to provide a home for her? To what degree have you gone out of your way to prepare to give your wife the things that will make her feel special and secure as your wife? Can two live as cheaply as one? Sure. If one doesn't eat and the other goes naked!

I'm not advocating that you have to be rich before you marry. If that had been a prerequisite, I'm not sure I would have ever won the hand of Teresa. My wife grew up the daughter of a man who did quite well in an oil exploration company. I was making only a whopping four hundred dollars a month! To my credit, I had a steady job and was a good steward of my income. I was also smart enough to find a young woman who had the same values toward money that I had. Through the years, it hasn't mattered how much or how little we have had—what has mattered to both of us is that we use our money wisely and for God's purposes.

Teresa knew that I was called by God into full-time ministry and that pastors are not rich people. She knew that she would never have all of the material things that her father could have given to her. She willingly accepted that reality, and I gratefully accepted her willingness. I did my best to provide for her an environment in which she wouldn't have to worry about where she would lay her head, whether she would have enough to eat, or whether the bills would be paid in full and on time. Even though we haven't been what one would call wealthy, we both are secure in the fact that I will provide for her to the best of my ability and that my best, along with our faith in God, will result in our having enough.

A woman desires to feel secure. She wants a man who is strong. Solomon provided not only sufficiency, but beauty for his wife. He gave her a clear expression of his best—not only his best character, but his best provision.

A groom who knows that he is strong inside in faith and character stands tall and proud. He is ready to assume the full responsibilities of marriage with deep, inner assurance that he desires to and can provide for his wife.

A GREAT WEDDING HAS PARENTAL APPROVAL

Great weddings are marked by approval of both sets of parents. In the Song of Solomon we read,

Go forth, O daughters of Zion,
And see King Solomon with the crown
With which his mother crowned him

The Wedding God Desires for You to Have

On the day of his wedding,
The day of the gladness of his heart. (Song 3:11)

Solomon's mother crowned him with the wedding crown that a groom wore in those days. It was a sign of her approval that he was marrying a woman she valued and would love as a daughter. It was also a sign to the general public that he would be leaving his parents' home and making a home of his own.

In that, Solomon's mother was glad, and Solomon was glad. There was a natural understanding of the truth first stated in Genesis 2:24: "Therefore a man shall leave his father and mother and be joined to his wife, and they shall become one flesh."

For centuries upon centuries, crowning was a part of marriage ceremonies. The bride was crowned with her veil, usually held in place by a heavily embroidered wedding cap or a crown of flowers. The wedding cap was perceived to be provided for her by her father—in essence, the father was crowning his daughter for marriage. The groom was crowned with a simple band of gold or with a garland of flowers, usually by his mother.

Today, the father continues to give the daughter's hand in marriage. The mother of the groom continues to weep silently as she gives up her son to another woman. Emotional heartstrings are involved in the same way they have been for centuries upon centuries.

The only thing that makes it truly possible for parents to give up their children to marriage is the belief that the marriage is God's plan. Their approval of a mate for their son or daughter is vital to overall family happiness, but also the happiness of the couple getting married.

While you are dating and courting, take time to get to know the family into which you will be marrying. You do not marry an isolated individual. You marry all of the people who are significant to that individual. You marry all of the childhood memories; you marry the values and beliefs instilled in the person by the family, including values about marriage and parenting.

If a husband or wife knows that family members are unsupportive and unappreciative, feelings of conflict, guilt, frustration, anger, bitterness, and resentment will likely arise. If you, in turn, are uncomfortable around the family members of your beloved, take this as a warning of troubled waters ahead. Discover the reasons for your lack of comfort. What unresolved issues are lurking just under the surface? In what ways are you going to have to deal with the dysfunction you perceive? Do long-standing problems exist that will continue to exist and affect your marriage relationship? Do you really want to deal with these problems?

The goal of every father and mother should be to raise their children not only to choose a godly spouse, but eventually to leave their care and make a home of their own. It is up to parents to be willing to let go. It is up to children to be willing to leave the nest. When parents are in approval of a marriage and are willing to let their children go emotionally and in areas of material and financial responsibility, and when children are willing to leave the security of their parents' love and provision, there is indeed a gladness to a wedding. This gladness of heart does not exist when parents resent or reject a future daughter-in-law or son-in-law, or when children continue to look to Dad and Mom for opinions, provision, security, and love more than they look to a spouse.

In some cases, the couple are not mature enough to "leave and cleave." At other times, the parents are not mature enough to let go. Both maturation processes need to be addressed in courtship so the wedding itself truly can become a day of release and a crowning.

For hundreds of years, those who married in traditional church ceremonies were crowned literally as part of the wedding ceremony, and then they walked around the canopy under which they recited their marriage vows as a regal walk—an open and full expression to all in attendance that they were the king and queen of their own home. This historical idea lingers in our culture today when we say that a man is "king of his castle" and a woman is "queen of her home." We see this tradition at most weddings as couples walk back down the aisle of the church together to the applause and cheers of an audience after they have been pronounced husband and wife.

Solomon was not only king of an empire on the day he married his beloved; he was the king of his *home.* His bride was not only the queen of his home; she was the queen of his *heart.*

A GREAT WEDDING SHOULD BE A DAY OF SPLENDOR

Solomon's wedding day was a day of pure splendor. Ceremony, preparation, symbolism, and faith came together in a time of holiness before the Lord. Two lives were joined as one spiritually, emotionally, financially, socially. Things had been done in right order, and there was a prevailing sense of "all is well" with the couple. That should be the description of your wedding too. You can make it so by making the right preparations during dating and courtship periods.

Was Solomon's wedding a romantic event? Was love in the air? You bet!

There is nothing more romantic than being able to look ahead or look back to your wedding day and say, "What a day of joy and blessing and goodness!" Your wedding day truly should be the highlight of your life—a day when all of God's plans for you come into focus, and all that you have experienced previously becomes only the prelude to the symphony of your future. Your wedding should be a day of loving bliss, great romance, and intimacy in emotion that is deep beyond words. Ask God to prepare you for that kind of wedding.

Questions to Think About or Discuss

1. *What spiritual symbols do you plan to have as part of your wedding ceremony? What do these symbols mean to you?*

2. *How do you feel about these statements: "God is a witness to your marriage vows" and "marriage is a sacred moment"?*

3. *Upon whom are you relying for emotional and spiritual support in your marriage?*

4. *What strengths are you bringing to your marriage?*

5. *What do you envision as the atmosphere or prevailing tone of your wedding?*

Five

The Honeymoon . . . at Last

Song of Solomon 4:1–5:1

I vividly recall the drive that my wife, Teresa, and I made from the church where we were married to the motel where we were to spend our wedding night. Mostly I recall that drive as a blur. I started out at the speed limit of sixty-five miles per hour, but the more we talked about the wedding being behind us and the honeymoon being before us, the faster I drove. Soon I was doing seventy-five miles an hour. And the more we talked, the more the pedal went to the metal, and the farther away she scooted. Finally I was doing about ninety miles per hour, and Teresa was clinging to the car door on her side, eyeing me warily! Predator and prey!

What a wonderful moment when you finally get to the honeymoon . . . at last. Couples tend to arrive at that moment exhilarated in their emotions, exhausted from the wedding, and energized by passion. They have made it in purity through what very likely have been years of dating, courtship, and engagement. They have experienced the holiness of a wonderful wedding ceremony. And now, all of the passion they have kept in check can be expressed.

As much as a couple may be eager for, excited about, and ready for sexual intimacy, questions and hesitations sometimes loom about sex. Ah, sex. It is the hope and desire of every young person. It is also one of life's greatest mysteries and secrets.

WHAT *DON'T* YOU KNOW ABOUT SEX?

Once upon a time there was a man who visited a community of people who lived by a river. As evening approached, he was invited to sit down by the river and enjoy a cool beverage and then dinner with the people. While they ate calmly and pleasantly, a fourteen-foot crocodile suddenly came up out of the river, chomped off the arm of the man sitting closest to the riverbank, and then slipped silently back into the dark waters. The people were alarmed and shocked, but they quickly recomposed themselves. Those closest to the man bandaged him up the best they could and transported him to medical assistance. Then they resumed their eating, drinking, and conversation—picking up right where they left off without any discussion of the incident.

The visiting man was horrified that the evening continued as if nothing had happened. Each time he tried to mention the tragic and violent act, someone in the group quickly changed the subject. He made one final attempt to bring the incident to discussion: "A man just lost his arm to an enormous crocodile that came suddenly out of the river. Didn't you all see that, or was I imagining things?"

Someone in the group replied, "Yes, we saw what happened. A number of people are attacked each year in our community by crocodiles."

The man then looked closer at the group and sure enough, he spotted people who were missing hands and feet, fingers and ears. "Can't you do anything about the crocodiles?" he asked.

Another in the group replied with embarrassment clearly written on his face, "It is impolite in our culture to talk about crocodiles."

The visitor to the community was stunned into bewildered silence.

At times I feel as he did when I see how the church deals with sex. So many people within the body of Christ seem to be wounded and maimed emotionally and psychologically by issues and problems related to sexual intimacy, and yet nobody in the church wants to discuss these issues. Sex is off-limits, something we just don't talk about in polite company, much less the holy company of fellow saints.

Where do most people learn about sex? On the wall of the rest room at the local gas station? On the playground? From a book or magazine that one discovers at a friend's house? From an R-rated movie?

Most of the information young people receive about sex does not come to them in a straightforward informational style, much less with an explanation about *why* a person should wait until marriage for sexual intercourse. Those who have sex education in the public school system are given factual and biological information, much of it about the physical mechanics of sex and the physical anatomy involved in reproduction, but they are not told the full truth about the emotional and psychological aspects of sexual intimacy. They are not given instruction as to the appropriate context for sexual intimacy. Information without moral context is a time bomb waiting to explode.

I know a number of parents who have fought vigorously to keep sex education out of the public school system, and some who have sought to keep sex education from being a part of the curriculum in their private Christian schools. Their reasoning is almost always the same: "We want the privilege as parents to tell our children about sex." But some of these same parents never seem to get around to having a straightforward, no-holds-barred, all-questions-appropriate-to-ask conversation in which sex is discussed fully, freely, and without embarrassment. Their version of sex education tends to be, "My advice is that you not do this until you are married." That's not much of an explanation to young people who want to know all of the what, when, where, why, how, and with whom details.

Planned Parenthood has determined from its polls that only 5 percent of the women who seek their services have ever had a parental conversation about sex. Even those parents who do prepare for sex-related talks with their children often discover that when they finally get around to having the discussion, they are a couple of years and a few experiences too late. I know of very few churches in which sex is discussed with youth groups or in Sunday school classes, much less from the pulpit.

And meanwhile, the crocodiles of inappropriate and ungodly sexual behavior are leaping out of the river of our society and taking giant chunks out of God's people. Emotions are being shattered, lives are being deeply impacted, and serious psychological scars are being formed—all for the want of lack of information and lack of understanding about God's plan for intimacy.

Thank God that we have His Word on the subject!

APPROACHING YOUR SPOUSE

In Solomon's era, the tradition regarding marriage was that the formal union of the couple happened in a public area, and then during the wedding reception, the bride and groom retired to a designated room where they consummated the marriage sexually. This custom has continued through the centuries, by the way, and still is the norm in many ultra-orthodox Jewish settings. When sexual intercourse was completed, it was then customary for the sheet on which the couple lay to be brought out for examination by the elders present at the wedding. They were looking for bloodstains that resulted from the virgin's hymen being penetrated. Bloodstains were considered a dual sign—the marriage had been consummated and the young woman indeed had been a virgin. If no blood appeared, the father of the bride could be in serious trouble because he could be charged with failing to maintain the virginity of his daughter. The dowry, monetary compensation, and sometimes an end to the marriage could all be brought into discussion at that point.

In Jewish cultures, once the marriage had been consummated, the couple might return to the wedding festivities to continue partying with their families and friends since wedding feasts often lasted a week or longer.

In the Song of Solomon, the bride and groom were alone, at last, in the bridal chamber. They were there for one purpose, and they both knew it. The bride still had on her veil and embroidered wedding cap to hold it in place. Solomon told her, "Behold, you are fair, my love! Behold, you are fair! You have dove's eyes behind your veil" (Song 4:1).

He was a smart man. He knew that sex for a woman always begins in her mind, a woman's most sensitive sexual organ. A woman doesn't feel the same pressure or insistent urges for sex that a man feels. She gets ready for sexual intimacy through what she thinks and feels, and to a great extent, she thinks and feels the way a man leads her to think and feel. Nothing calms a woman's fears and excites her passions as much as having a man tell her how wonderful she is. The man told the woman, who just a couple of chapters ago was complaining about her dark skin, how fair she was to him. He liked what he saw, and he told her so. He appreciated her, valued her, acknowledged her beauty, built her up. And he looked deep into her eyes as he spoke. It was a wonderfully intimate moment between the two newly married people. He looked into her soul as a prelude to exploring her body. Solomon has been called the wisest man who ever lived, and in this moment, he exhibited wisdom. He knew how to reach the innermost depths of the woman he had married.

He then began to undress her, starting with her wedding cap. As he removed it from her, the locks of her hair tumbled down freely and sensuously. Many Jewish women have very curly hair, and that is the image depicted here. The locks of her hair were a little wild, a little disheveled, cascading down over her shoulders, just like a flock of goats playfully skipping down the mountains of Gilead. The mountains, on the east side of the Jordan, were known for their excellent grazing land. They were considered a blessing and were occupied by countless flocks and herds. The image is that the man was nuzzling the hair of the woman, his face fully into her long curly locks of hair.

Next came the removal of her wedding veil so that Solomon for the first time had a full view of the face of the woman he had married. In our culture today we would find this nearly unthinkable that a man might marry a woman whose face he had never seen fully. Yet that was customary in Solomon's time, and in fact, is still the custom in a number of very strict Muslim communities. A woman's beauty in those communities is considered to be solely for her husband's pleasure—he is the only man apart from her brothers and father who really knows what she looks like. A man is not allowed the privilege we American men have of shopping around for a wife like customers staring into store windows.

Solomon began to tell her that he liked what he saw. And the good news was that she was responding to him with a wonderful open-mouthed smile of pleasure. How do we know that? Because he complimented her teeth. He said,

> *Your teeth are like a flock of shorn sheep*
> *Which have come up from the washing,*
> *Every one of which bears twins,*
> *And none is barren among them.* (Song 4:2)

You and I might not consider that to be a compliment. If a man came to a woman today and said, "Your teeth are like a flock of shorn sheep," the woman would likely feel more offended than complimented. Solomon was noting that she had a marvelous smile, and that her white, even, straight mouth full of teeth was a delight to him. It spoke to him that she had taken care of herself and hadn't been subjected to disease, abuse, or injury. It spoke to him of her delicacy and her genteel manner. I don't know of too many women who would desire a compliment on their teeth, but I don't know of any woman who doesn't delight to hear the man she loves say to her, "I love your smile. I love the sound of your laughter." Solomon appreciated her beautiful soul, her beautiful features, and her beautiful expression of joy.

Teeth are part of the mouth, of course, and Solomon was moving in for a kiss. He continued, "Your lips are like a strand of scarlet, and your mouth is lovely" (Song 4:3). This is kissing talk. He was tracing her features with his hands, but also likely tracing them with his mouth as he whispered his approval and appreciation to her: "Your temples behind your veil are like a piece of pomegranate" (Song 4:3).

She was blushing! He liked that. He could tell she was starting to tingle at his touch and respond to his close presence. He moved on down from her face to her neck and said,

Your neck is like the tower of David,
Built for an armory,
On which hang a thousand bucklers,
All shields of mighty men. (Song 4:4)

The woman was standing tall and straight before Solomon—no shame, no bowed head in disgrace. She had an inner strength of character that matched his own. She knew who she was, and as his new bride, she knew who she was in relationship with him. She was not embarrassed by what he was doing, and neither was she rigid under his gaze or his touch. Rather, she was ready for all that he had to say to her. She had a tilt to her head and a sparkle in her eyes, ready for him to explore her further. Such is the unashamed beauty of sexuality in its divine setting.

This bride might have been wearing a necklace that Solomon was undoing as he spoke those words. The "tower of David" was a military structure, and the mighty men in David's army hung their shields on its exterior during peace times. It was a dramatic expression to all the people in the land that David was prepared for war but was presently at peace. Women's necklaces at that time were often made of coins or hammered flat pieces of metal, row upon row like a multiple strand of pearls. The woman's necklace might very well have looked like David's tower, and she might very well have been like all that the tower symbolized—ready to spring into action to defend what she knew to be hers, and equally ready to be at complete peace with the man she loved.

Notice that up to that point a great deal of sensuality and romance had been going on. The man didn't just jump out of his chariot and into the bedsheets of the closest motel and overwhelm the woman with his desire for her. He dealt with her tenderly, spoke to her, kissed her, made her feel special and desirable. He built a desire for himself within her mind and heart. He was being *romantic.*

There is an old, but true, saying: men give romance to get sex; women give sex to get romance. Solomon was doing the right thing by his bride.

What is romance? Most people don't know what the word means or how it came into being.

During the times of the Roman Empire when Latin was the *lingua franca*—the official common language for all of the conquered peoples of the Western world—all formal documents were written in Latin, from wedding certificates to coroners' reports to documents related to proclamations, historic events, and battles.

When the common people spoke, however, of love and poetry and heroism and chivalry, they did not use classic Latin; rather, they used what was called the vulgar tongue. It was the language common to a certain geographic area. It was the language used by the average man in daily conversation. The languages from the area eventually came to be called the Romance languages. They were the languages used for the telling of love stories and tales of chivalry, bravery, and valor. The term *romantic,* therefore, referred to informal talking and passion as opposed to formal writing and legal transactions.

Men, when you marry, you will sign a wedding license, and you will have a formal "Latin" relationship with your wife. You will be expected to be the family breadwinner, provide the life insurance, give all you can to your family, and take care of your wife until death parts you from each other. But your marriage, if it remains only a "Latin" relationship, will be sterile, boring, and rigid. A woman longs for the lingua franca of passion and romance. Solomon knew that, and he used "romance talk." He spoke to his bride in terms that she knew and appreciated, and to which she responded with sexual ardor. That's right—a good marriage has a degree of "vulgarity."

BUILDING PASSION AND DESIRE

Gary Smalley wrote, "Men are microwaves, women are Crock-Pots." He's right, as far as I'm concerned. A man can have sex just about any time and appreciate it in just about any form. A woman, however, heats up slowly. She needs time and tenderness to be ready for sexual intercourse.

Men as a whole seem to be able to appreciate sex as long as they are shown some appreciation and are given a green light. Women, in contrast, have a difficult time appreciating sex if it is completely void of kindness, appreciation, and gentleness.

That's the way God made us. Men and women are different. If women had the sex drives of men, nothing would get done. The entire world would be having sex all the time. If men had the sex drives of women, we wouldn't have a population problem.

Solomon was engaged in slow, romantic foreplay with the woman he loved. He moved down from her neck to her breasts, saying, "Your two breasts are like two fawns, twins of a gazelle, which feed among the lilies" (Song 4:5).

Solomon was undressing his bride and expressing appreciation for everything he saw before him. Fawns are young, sweet, and tender—baby gazelles. As I mentioned before, the gazelle is a sleek and graceful animal, very youthful in appearance—lean and taut and always on the alert. The woman's breasts were youthful in every way. And Solomon treated her just as a person would approach a new fawn—touching her breasts tenderly so as not to frighten or overwhelm her. His touch was gentle. He was moving slowly and cautiously.

That's a good strategy for every man to take, especially on his wedding night. A guy I knew in college told me about his experience with his wife. He married a girl who had never been kissed before he kissed her. She was extremely inexperienced and shy. He, on the other hand, had fantasized just about every fantasy a guy can come up with, and he was ready to experience all of his fantasies the first night. He told me he came roaring out of the bathroom of their hotel room on their wedding night as if he were Conan the Barbarian and poured out all of his passion on her. He said, "I scared her to death, and it took years of counseling for her to begin to open up and truly appreciate her passion and sexuality."

Men and women tend to have different parameters about what they consider to be appropriate sexual behavior. How far can a man go? As far as he wants as long as his wife doesn't feel demeaned in the process. If a woman has a problem with a specific sexual act or position, then a man needs to stop immediately.

When I conduct premarital counseling sessions, I make couples talk about what they believe is appropriate sexual behavior. I ask, "How would you feel about this? What about that?" Some of the couples are embarrassed, but they generally admit to me later that this is a very helpful part of our counseling time. It's better to give some serious thought to what you like and don't like, what you'd like to try and not try, and so forth before your wedding night.

It's also important that both persons be willing to experiment and be flexible to the greatest degree possible in their thinking when it comes to sexual behavior. Sexual intimacy is not a formula. Some men discover that their wives respond to certain types of kisses and strokes more than to others, and they work up a little formula: "Do this, touch there, stroke here, kiss again, and so forth." And generally speaking, these men are shocked when their formula doesn't work one night.

Sexual behavior is intended to have an element of spontaneity, surprise, and experimentation to it. It is neither a prescription nor a recipe. A man needs to approach his wife with an awareness that she is a wonderfully creative human being who is subject to changes, whims, emotional highs and lows, and sudden shifts in mood. He is expressing love to a living, vibrant, ever-growing, and ever-changing creature.

Over time, a man will learn certain signals that tell him his wife is approachable. Watch for them. Some couples experience frustration in this area because they don't have enough signals. One man told me that he knew whether his wife would be interested in having sex that night by what she wore when she came out of the bathroom and climbed into bed. If she was wearing a slinky nightgown, she was in the mood. If she was wearing flannel pajamas, she wasn't. One woman said to me, "It's in the aftershave. If he's wearing aftershave, then I know he wants sex."

Let me share with you a couple of verses of Scripture that I encourage women to memorize and I admonish men never to quote:

> *The wife does not have authority over her own body, but the husband does. And likewise the husband does not have authority over his own body, but the wife does. Do not deprive one another except with consent for a time, that you may give yourselves to fasting and prayer; and come together again so that Satan does not tempt you because of your lack of self-control.* (1 Cor. 7:4–5)

Let's deal with the last part of this scriptural passage first. The only time you should deny each other sexual pleasure is when, *by mutual agreement,* you have set aside a specific and designated time for concentrated fasting and prayer. As soon as that time is over, a normal sexual pattern should resume.

And now for the first part of this passage. Paul knew what men for thousands of years have known. Women do not have the same physical need for sex that men have. There are going to be times in a marriage when a wife must honor her husband by having sex with him in order to satisfy a physical need in his body. There will be times when a husband knows that his wife is only having sex with him because she believes it is the loving and right thing to do; her heart and emotions really aren't fully desirous of sex in the way he is. According to Paul, there are also times when a wife may feel a need for sex and her husband may not feel that same need. I don't know too many men who fit that description, but apparently such men exist, and in those cases, a husband needs to honor the need of his wife and give her the sexual satisfaction that she desires. The main point Paul was making is this: wives must put the needs of their husbands before their own needs, and husbands must put the needs of their wives above their own needs. Each must give sacrificially and generously to the other, in sexual behavior and in all other ways in a marriage. Marriage is mostly about giving, not receiving. Only the holy and selfless can truly be great lovers.

Years ago, young women in England were instructed that on their wedding night, they should lie on their backs and think of the queen, meaning that they were to endure sex so that they might conceive babies who would be loyal citizens to the queen and loyal soldiers in her army. What a terrible image! What an unfortunate lack of pleasure for women and for the men who had sex with them.

Thank goodness, the Song of Solomon gives us a much different impression of sex. The Lord desires for His people to experience joyful and mutual sharing and giving.

ALL NIGHT WITH HIS BELOVED

Solomon had this to say about his lovemaking to his bride:

> *Until the day breaks*
> *And the shadows flee away,*
> *I will go my way to the mountain of myrrh*
> *And to the hill of frankincense.* (Song 4:6)

He made love to his bride all night long. Their passion lasted until dawn. The "mountain" and "hill" could be the "hills of separation" in Song of Solomon 2—a reference to her breasts. Or they could be a combined idea of her breasts being the mountain and her genital area the hill. Either way, he was intoxicated with the delights of his wife!

Appreciating His Bride's Body

In the opening chapter of the Song of Solomon, the woman said to Solomon, "Do not look upon me, because I am dark, because the sun has tanned me" (Song 1:6). What did Solomon say to her after they experienced a night of sexual bliss? "You are all fair, my love, and there is no spot in you" (Song 4:7). He appreciated her body. He praised her appearance and let her know that he found no fault in her.

One of the most painful things a man can ever do to his bride is to see her disrobed for the first time and then say something disparaging about her body. That deep hurt is likely to be one she never forgets. All women tend to be self-conscious about their bodies, and my wife has advised me that every woman has something about her body she would like to change.

Young man, your bride may not be a supermodel in appearance. But she is *your* bride. She doesn't need for you to tell her she is the most beautiful creature in all the world. She'll recognize that as a con and a lie a mile away. She needs to hear that she pleases you, and that as far as you are concerned, she is perfect in your eyes. A woman who truly feels cherished by her husband in all ways is going to give herself to her husband freely and generously. Remember that our heavenly Bridegroom sees us as being without "spot or wrinkle." (See Eph. 5.)

Moving Toward a Mutual Climax

Solomon continued in his passionate lovemaking:

> *Come with me from Lebanon, my spouse,*
> *With me from Lebanon.*
> *Look from the top of Amana,*
> *From the top of Senir and Hermon,*
> *From the lions' dens,*
> *From the mountains of the leopards.* (Song 4:8)

Solomon was calling to his wife to move from the lowlands where the lions roamed to the mountaintops where the leopards lived. It is a clear description of sexual climax—moving higher and higher to the greatest emotional ecstasy possible. He wanted her not only to be one with him in a physical union, but also to experience the same ecstasy that he was experiencing. He desired for his wife to experience the same release in orgasm that he was about to experience. She was his sexual partner not his plaything. Another interpretation of this text is that Solomon is calling his bride away from everything in life that is frightening to the safety of his love. Or he is urging her to leave her life and become part of a new family. Such is the union that sexual oneness brings.

He continued,

> *You have ravished my heart,*
> *My sister, my spouse;*

You have ravished my heart
With one look of your eyes,
With one link of your necklace.
How fair is your love,
My sister, my spouse!
How much better than wine is your love,
And the scent of your perfumes
Than all spices!
Your lips, O my spouse,
Drip as the honeycomb;
Honey and milk are under your tongue;
And the fragrance of your garments
Is like the fragrance of Lebanon. (Song 4:9–11)

Everything about these three verses speaks of the most intense passion possible. His heart was beating faster and faster. He was kissing her deeply—what we would call a French kiss although it was nineteen hundred years before France was a nation. It was a genuine Hebrew kiss, deep and penetrating. Open-mouth kisses are one of the most sensual acts possible in a marriage union. Solomon was kissing her deeply and intimately.

And then the shift was suddenly to the fact that the woman was still a virgin. Solomon declared it to be so as if he was discovering in their very act of lovemaking that she was a virgin:

A garden enclosed
Is my sister, my spouse,
A spring shut up,
A fountain sealed. (Song 4:12)

In the Bible a man's sexuality is described as a spring; a woman's sexuality is described as a well. Solomon was stating very plainly that the woman had not experienced a man's "spring" within her; her fountain had been sealed off. Her hymen had not been broken. What an exaltation of purity and virginity. How honoring Solomon had been to their sexual limits! But now was the time for that to change:

> *Your plants are an orchard of pomegranates*
> *With pleasant fruits,*
> *Fragrant henna with spikenard,*
> *Spikenard and saffron,*
> *Calamus and cinnamon,*
> *With all trees of frankincense,*
> *Myrrh and aloes,*
> *With all the chief spices—*
> *A fountain of gardens,*
> *A well of living waters,*
> *And streams from Lebanon.* (Song 4:13–15)

The woman was fragrant and moist in her sexual passion as he was reaching sexual climax within her. Their union was complete. Solomon was in his garden.

For some time, the woman had been told not to awaken her passions until she could experience them fully. ("Do not stir up nor awaken love until it pleases" is a twice-given admonition in earlier chapters.) Now, what did the woman say?

> *Awake, O north wind,*
> *And come, O south!*
> *Blow upon my garden,*
> *That its spices may flow out.*
> *Let my beloved come to his garden*
> *And eat its pleasant fruits.* (Song 4:16)

The north winds are strong; the south winds are gentle. The woman wanted to be awakened completely in all her passion. She wanted to experience all of love there was to experience, and she wanted her husband to experience her fully. She delighted in sexual intimacy with her husband.

A young bride asked me as she sat in the bridal room awaiting the wedding ceremony, "Pastor Tommy, what do I do?" She was wide-eyed and a little scared. Suddenly she was facing the fact that within a few hours, she and her beloved young groom were going to be alone together and embarking on an experience of sexual intimacy. I thought to myself, *Now is not the time to be having this conversation!*

I said to her, "Whatever you are feeling, tell him." That was the best advice I could give her at the time, and in retrospect, I have concluded that it was very good advice. A wife needs to respond to her husband by telling him what she likes and doesn't like, how she's feeling, and what she desires to feel even more strongly. Solomon's bride had no trouble in saying to her husband what she wanted. She said, in effect, "Come and have all the sex you want. Come to my garden and eat your fill of my fruit." She turned it loose.

If I had been able to think fast enough in that moment of crash counseling, I would have also told that young bride, "Consider that every part of you is free and available to your husband. Let him explore all of you." A man is energized sexually by what he sees and what he feels. If nothing is withheld, he withholds nothing. Solomon's bride was holding nothing back.

Great sex to a woman is tenderness. To a man, it's responsiveness. The couple had deeply met their mutual needs.

IN THE AFTERMATH OF SEXUAL UNION

As the fifth chapter of the Song of Solomon opens, the couple had had their fill of lovemaking. Solomon was lying on his back, sighing deeply no doubt, as he said,

I have come to my garden, my sister, my spouse;
I have gathered my myrrh with my spice;
I have eaten my honeycomb with my honey;
I have drunk my wine with my milk. (Song 5:1)

Nine times Solomon called the woman "mine." Such is biblical sex. The two were now one.

He was completely satisfied. He expressed a complete release of his passion. He was resting in bliss. In that euphoria Solomon called out in his spirit to those outside the bridal chamber, waiting for his emergence: "Eat, O friends! Drink, yes, drink deeply, O beloved ones!" (Song 5:1).

Some believe this is the voice of God, saying to the couple, "Enjoy My gift." God indeed delights in what delights us. Others believe that Solomon was saying, in effect, "Party on, my friends. Have a second helping of the hors d'oeuvres. Have another glass of wine—in fact, have several. I'm going to be here a while. I'm in no hurry to put an end to this experience, and you'll just have to be patient. You aren't going to be seeing me anytime soon." His beloved bride had invited him to come into her garden and eat to his heart's delight, and Solomon was more than willing to do just that! He was full and relaxing in the pleasure he had experienced.

When sexual intimacy occurs in right timing and with the right person, from God's perspective, it is meant to be enjoyed fully. Sex under an alias—in a dark corner, a backseat, or a motel, with a person other than your spouse—is never sex that can be enjoyed to the maximum because there will always be an element of guilt and shame associated with it.

Once you are with your beloved, however, and within the vows of holy matrimony, sex is meant to be a source of pleasure for both the man and the woman. There should be no sense of shame or guilt. Obviously that was the case for

Solomon and his bride. They were enjoying each other immensely. While their friends were partying, they, too, were engaged in their own private party, drinking deeply of their passion and sexuality. To those who think the Bible is against sex: on your most passionate nights you will not approach the romance, tenderness, and passion of biblical, holy sexuality.

Ah, yes, the honeymoon at last!

Questions to Think About or Discuss

1. *What issues related to sex do you find difficult to discuss with your beloved?*

2. *What more do you wish you knew about sexual intimacy? To whom do you intend to go to gain this information?*

Six

Conflicts

Song of Solomon 5:2–6:3

Back in the early 1980s, my wife, Teresa, and I were in Oklahoma City where I had been invited to conduct a wedding ceremony. My wife stayed in our motel room the morning after the wedding while I went out for a jog. It was hot and humid, and by the time I finished my run, my T-shirt was soaked with sweat. I came back into our motel room, stripped off my T-shirt, and threw it in a nearby paper bag—which is obviously where I thought such a garment ought to go. My wife reacted instantly without thinking.

She whopped me with her right hand across the middle of my back and said, "Don't do that!" *Bam!* I was stunned by her reaction and just as quickly turned and said sharply, "Cut that out!" My harsh words caused tears to well in her eyes immediately. I felt wronged, and she felt wronged by being yelled at. I didn't know that she had put a new dress that she was sewing into that paper bag, and she didn't know that I didn't know.

And there we were, just hours after my performing a ceremony of holy matrimony, with a joyous reception afterward, getting into our car and driving toward Texarkana in angry silence, far from the ideal of the happily married couple that I had advocated publicly. We drove five hours without a word between us, and then neither of us could stand the silence any longer. We began to communicate about what had really happened and why each had felt wronged. By the time we finally arrived at our destination, we had forgiven each other and were ready to kiss and make up.

All couples fight. Good couples fight clean. Bad couples fight dirty.

Good conflict leads to a resolution in which both parties feel peace, and a new platform for communication and cooperation is established between them. Bad conflict leads to a victory for one and a loss for the other, which results in some degree of hidden resentment and bitterness that are stored away for a future fight.

Good marital conflict leads to resolution and greater closeness. Bad marital conflict presses for victory, which leads to alienation and the potential for revenge.

EVERY MARRIAGE HAS CONFLICT

No marriage is without conflict. Frankly, a marriage without any conflict would be very boring. There likely would be a lack of deep or meaningful communication. Such a marriage might as well be a butler married to a maid, each of whom is reluctant to express his or her personality, dreams, desires, goals, or spiritual giftedness. A truly vibrant marriage is going to be marked by discussion—at times lively. Healthy disagreements arise naturally because both individuals maintain their unique perspectives, ideas, and opinions. Debate is common about which course of action to take, since each person has individual preferences and reasons for holding them.

Discussion, disagreement, and debate, however, do not need to degenerate into a cold war or an ongoing atmosphere of dispute. Discussions should reach a conclusion, disagreements should resolve into agreement, and debates should come to a decisive course of action. Marriages without conflict aren't healthy and growing. All married couples, therefore, face the challenge of learning to fight clean and fair, with a positive outcome that is genuinely harmonious, not merely strained and silent.

Newly married couples need to expect conflict, although I am not advocating that they should look for it. Picking a fight just for the sake of having a fight is not the goal. At the same time, a husband or wife should never shy away from conflict in a spirit of denial—either denying oneself full expression of opinions and ideas, or denying that certain situations within the marriage need resolution, repair, or readdressing. Those who live in denial live in false peace.

It is far better to get differences of opinion out in the open than to keep them stuffed inside for the sake of perceived peace. Such peace is going to be fragile. Feelings of anger and hurt are likely to go underground and build to an explosion point at a later time. Too much pent-up emotion related to any issue can cause a situation to be blown far beyond the proportions warranted by the initial behavior or circumstance.

One person I know said this about his marriage of twenty-five years to a wife he adores: "Neither of us is good at silence. We vent our feelings frequently. We are quick to state our opinions and quick to resolve our differences. We don't let anything negative brew and build between us. If we ever let things build up in us over time, we'd likely blow ourselves up in the process of blowing off steam."

In my opinion, this couple has a very healthy attitude toward conflict.

Marriage Is Worth Some Conflict

One of the strangest verses in the entire Bible must be Proverbs 14:4: "Where no oxen are, the trough is clean; but much increase comes by the strength of an ox."

The verse means that if you don't have any oxen, you will obviously have a clean manger or feeding trough. You may be happy to have a clean trough, which doesn't require any work, but on the other hand, you are likely to be much happier if you have oxen in your stable. Strong oxen enable much work to get done—many acres plowed, cultivated, and harvested. Strong oxen lead to great increase in the field. You will probably desire to have a "dirty" trough and its related work because the presence of oxen means more prosperity down the line.

The same principle holds true for a marriage. If you aren't married, you may very well have less conflict in your life. But if you want the deep joys of having a spouse and children, you will gladly endure conflict as part of the price for having a family.

THREE STAGES OF MARRIAGE

Conflict usually is minimal during the first stage of a marriage, which is the *honeymoon period. Honeymoon* literally refers to a "sweet month." It marks the period from one stage of the moon to the next time that stage of the moon occurs (a full month) and also to a month in the spring of the year (usually May or June). During these spring months, flowers, shrubs, and trees bloom most profusely in most regions of the Northern Hemisphere, and the honeybees can be about their work with much productivity. In a marriage, the honeymoon period is the period of sweetness and kindness between two spouses, a time when all things seem new and fresh and exciting—about thirty days.

The next stage of a marriage, however, is often called the *disillusionment period*—when illusions about the person you have married disappear. A woman thinks she has married

Ozzie Nelson, and he turns out to be Homer Simpson. A man thinks he has married the girl of his dreams and awakens to hard, glaring reality.

After the disillusionment period comes the wonderful and long-enduring phase of *commitment,* when you discover your mate fully and, at the same time, commit to loving your mate in a biblical manner for the rest of your days.

Both the disillusionment and the commitment phases are going to be marked by conflict, and since they are by far the longer periods of time for a marriage, partners are wise to anticipate these periods prior to their wedding and set their minds and hearts to enduring the disillusionment period in anticipation of the commitment phase. Determine going into your honeymoon that you *will* survive the impending disillusionment phase. At the same time, refuse to shy away from conflict during your dating, courtship, and engagement periods. Keep your discussions and conversations lively. Don't "stuff" your emotions in fear that you will damage your relationship. Learn to fight fair.

SIX STAGES OF CONFLICT

The inevitability of conflict is addressed in the Song of Solomon. Nearly two chapters are devoted to a "fight" between Solomon and his bride. The result of the conflict was a deeper and better marriage, and therefore, we are going to take a close look at the six stages of their conflict.

STAGE ONE: BOTH PARTIES FEEL HARMED

Conflict occurs when both parties feel in some way wronged, denied, misunderstood, or unappreciated. We find a perfect example in the conflict between Solomon and his bride:

> *I sleep, but my heart is awake;*
> *It is the voice of my beloved!*
> *He knocks, saying,*
> *"Open for me, my sister, my love,*
> *My dove, my perfect one;*
> *For my head is covered with dew,*
> *My locks with the drops of the night."* (Song 5:2)

Solomon had been working late. He came home, drenched with the dew of the early morning, and he was eager to get home to his wife. Like many men, he was struggling in the hard, cruel world, and he longed to come home to some tenderness and appreciation.

In those days, a man and a woman often had different bedchambers. Solomon was knocking at the door of his wife's room so that he might come into her bedroom and be with her, lie under the sheets in her embrace, and talk over his day with her. He was seeking both emotional and physical intimacy with his wife. He needed her at the end of the day.

She, on the other hand, had pretty much given up on his coming home at a reasonable hour and had gone to bed. She said to him, "I was asleep, but my heart"—which referred to Solomon, the object of her love—"was awake." His voice was intrusive into her peaceful dreams. Then she added,

> *I have taken off my robe;*
> *How can I put it on again?*
> *I have washed my feet;*
> *How can I defile them?* (Song 5:3)

Her response, in modern-day terms, might be, "I have a headache." She said in poetic terms, "Not tonight. I'm already in bed, and now you want me to get up and get dressed and open the door to you? No way." She said, "I've already taken a bath. Yet you want to have sex now?"

My wife has a little saying that she sometimes recites when someone in our family exhibits selfish behavior. It goes, "Me, me, me, I love myself. I have my picture on my shelf." That was the way the woman responded to Solomon. She had little regard for his need or desire. She didn't care how hard he worked or how much he needed her. She put her needs before his. She was feeling wronged by Solomon: "I waited up for you, but now it's way past midnight. If you can't get yourself home at a decent hour, don't expect special attention from me." It should be noted that it is possible to have a torrid honeymoon, and yet shortly thereafter, find that to the woman, sex has become a duty.

Solomon persisted in his expression of desire and longing for her:

> *My beloved put his hand*
> *By the latch of the door,*
> *And my heart yearned for him.*
> *I arose to open for my beloved,*
> *And my hands dripped with myrrh,*
> *My fingers with liquid myrrh,*
> *On the handles of the lock.*
> *I opened for my beloved,*
> *But my beloved had turned away and was gone.* (Song 5:4–6)

At that point, Solomon was also feeling wronged. His wife rebuffed him.

Solomon didn't break the door down or demand entrance. He didn't press the point. He reached out to her in sincerity and tenderness. He spoke sweetly and lovingly to her. The myrrh that he left on the latch was a symbol of sweetness. His attitude toward her was tender.

When he got no response, Solomon walked away. He no doubt felt rejected. He might very well have said under his breath, "Hey, I'm the king. I married you. I've loved you. I've given you the family checkbook. I do my best to provide for all your needs. I was working late at my job tonight, I came to you in a loving manner, and look what I get. You have rejected me. I don't deserve this response from you."

Two persons feeling wronged—that's the first part of any conflict. If only one person feels wronged and then thinks through the situation and concludes, "Actually I haven't been all that wronged or hurt," an argument or disagreement is not likely to occur. But when both spouses feel that a wrong has been done to them, conflict ensues.

At this stage of feeling wronged a conflict can be most easily resolved. How? You can determine that you do not need to react as your mate has reacted. If your mate has hurt you, you do not need to hurt your mate. Whatever your mate has done to you, you do not need to respond in kind. The apostle Paul stated it this way: "See that no one renders evil for evil to anyone, but always pursue what is good both for yourselves and for all" (1 Thess. 5:15).

You do not have to reciprocate or mirror what others do to you or say about you. Your mother probably taught this principle to you in the way my mother taught me: "Two wrongs do not make a right."

Your response is subject to your will. You do not need to be hateful, angry, or cruel to a person who hurts you. You can respond with the love and patience of the Spirit of God rather than the revengeful and impatient spirit of man.

Strife begins at the point when you allow yourself to have

hurt feelings and then you choose to nurse that hurt and wallow in it. Proverbs speaks often on this subject:

> *A wrathful man stirs up strife,*
> *But he who is slow to anger allays contention.* (Prov. 15:18)
>
> *He who is slow to anger is better than the mighty,*
> *And he who rules his spirit than he who takes a city.*
> (Prov. 16:32)
>
> *Better is a dry morsel with quietness,*
> *Than a house full of feasting with strife.* (Prov. 17:1)
>
> *The beginning of strife is like releasing water;*
> *Therefore stop contention before a quarrel starts.* (Prov. 17:14)
>
> *The north wind brings forth rain,*
> *And a backbiting tongue an angry countenance.*
> *It is better to dwell in a corner of a housetop,*
> *Than in a house shared with a contentious woman.*
> (Prov. 25:23–24)
>
> *Where there is no wood, the fire goes out;*
> *And where there is no talebearer, strife ceases.*
> *As charcoal is to burning coals, and wood to fire,*
> *So is a contentious man to kindle strife.* (Prov. 26:20–21)
>
> *An angry man stirs up strife,*
> *And a furious man abounds in transgression.* (Prov. 29:22)

You may be saying, "But you said, Tommy, that I should not stifle my feelings and that I should express them freely in my marriage." That's absolutely correct, but how and when you express your feelings, and with what underlying motive and attitude, are very important.

Express yourself, yes, but wait until your emotional temperature has cooled. Be proactive and intentional, not reactive and instinctual, in expressing your feelings. Wait until the one who has hurt you also has cooled off or is in a good frame of mind to hear what you have to say.

In the instance that I cited at the beginning of this chapter, Teresa later said to me that she realized she should have let me go on to the shower, removed my sweaty T-shirt from the bag, and about halfway to Texarkana brought up the incident and said, "You know, Tommy, I am sewing a new dress, and I had put it in that paper bag where you threw your sweaty T-shirt. I would appreciate it in the future if you would look before you blindly throw your sweaty garments into a bag. I know you would never want to damage my sewing. Please be a little more cautious, okay, Honey?"

I would have bent over backward to accommodate such a request. Of course, I didn't want to damage her sewing.

There have been conflicts in which I should have bridled my tongue, too, or not taken steps that amounted to retaliation. Every person I know can do a better job of keeping a cool head and choosing at all times to respond as Christ would respond. It's tough to do, but it's what we as Christians are called and challenged by God to do.

I know people who have grown up in homes where passive-aggressive behavior was the norm. That's behavior in which a person is warm and loving one minute, and the next minute, the person is ice cold or hateful. One day everything seems to be flowing smoothly, the following day an argument erupts, and for the next two weeks, everybody in the household walks about on eggshells because Mom and Dad are "at it" again.

Such behavior does not need to occur. Conflict can be resolved at this very first stage if one of the persons in the relationship will be mature enough to sit back, analyze and pray about the situation, and make a measured response that is loving, kind, and aimed at a greater positive in the future.

Be Sensitive to Arising Conflict

A number of people who have heard me teach on the Song of Solomon have asked me, "But how can I tell if my spouse is upset over something I've done? My spouse doesn't seem to give me any clue that I've stepped on her toes or tripped her up." Every person has different means of communicating and sending signals. It may take you a little time to determine when you have overstepped the boundaries of what your mate considers to be appropriate or good behavior. My wife's foremost clue to me is a little look that she gives me, ever so fleetingly, in which she communicates volumes: "With behavior like that, you're not worth being around." I'm more verbal. I sigh *very* deeply and loudly enough for her to hear me. And then I tend to go immediately to a chair and pick up my Bible and begin reading it. If she asks me what I'm doing, I say, "I'm drawing strength from God to live in an alien and hostile world." She gets the point. I do, too, every time she gives me that certain withering look.

They are the cues we give to each other to say, "Let's each take stock of what has just happened here." Ideally we'll replay in our minds what has happened, draw some conclusions, and come together at a later time for a rational, unheated discussion.

What fuels a conflict rather than defuses it is the attitude, "I'm walking away from you until you get your act together and are repentant." A cooling-off period is not the same as assuming a cold, unresponsive, punishing attitude. A cooling-off period does not need to be precipitated by a loud stomping off or the tossing of a final barb over one's shoulder.

A Continued Pursuit in Love

Solomon did not at first respond to his wife's rejection in an angry way. He persisted in expressing his desire. At first he only called to her. She heard his voice. Then even after she had rejected him verbally, he reached out for her. His behavior did not mirror hers. He continued to pursue her in love.

Refuse to overreact or to react too quickly to what another person does or says. One person said to me, "My mother had a phrase, 'Let the river roll on for a while.' We lived near a river, and I knew precisely what she meant. Some things are best left to float right on by because they are issues that are too little to warrant a fight." You might have heard it said, "Don't make mountains out of mole hills." Same principle. Continue to pursue your relationship and your spouse with love. Don't make big issues out of little ones. Proverbs 12:16 tells us, "A fool's wrath is known at once, but a prudent man covers shame."

How does this square with my earlier advice that you not let certain things build up inside you until you feel an explosion coming on? Very easily. It is up to you to give weight to a situation or circumstance that you perceive to be a conflict. Some things are not worthy of emotional battles or open conflict. Other things that should be addressed need to be addressed in the right time and place, with the right attitude and goal. It is up to you to decide what really matters. Choose your areas for discussion and conflict resolution wisely.

Maintain your poise and composure when you feel hurt, rejected, or maligned by someone. Choose to take control over your attitude and to control the subsequent discussion of the issue with a tone of quietness and positive communication.

Peter taught,

> *Wives, likewise, be submissive to your own husbands. . . . Do not let your adornment be merely outward . . . rather let it be the*

> *hidden person of the heart, with the incorruptible beauty of a gentle and quiet spirit, which is very precious in the sight of God. . . . Husbands, likewise, dwell with them with understanding, giving honor to the wife, as to the weaker vessel, and as being heirs together of the grace of life, that your prayers may not be hindered. Finally, all of you be of one mind, having compassion for one another.* (1 Peter 3:1, 3–4, 7–8)

Peter encouraged wives and husbands to deal with each other graciously and tenderly. A wife is to bear a gentle and quiet spirit in her discussions with her husband. A husband is to approach his wife as if she is as delicate as a china cup—which is what it means to regard a wife as a "weaker" vessel—recognizing that his bombastic tone and mannerisms can cause his wife to shrivel inside and to feel demeaned.

Don't hurt each other, Peter said. Have compassion for each other, and seek to have one mind—in other words, love each other until you reach a common point of agreement.

Such an attitude and means of resolving a conflict begin with how you individually choose to respond to a situation. Will you allow your hurt to linger, fester, and grow, or will you give it to the Lord, ask for His help in resolving the situation, and then speak to your spouse later in lovingkindness and with a sure and sincere approach that can bring you to positive resolution?

We come to know in our marriages when we have hurt a spouse. There is a look in the eyes, a slumping of the shoulders, a slow walk away, or a spirit of dejection. I know immediately when I have hurt Teresa. Her eyes fill with tears and I know that—regardless of what has been said or done, and regardless of how "right" I might have been in what I did—I must ask her forgiveness first for hurting her. She knows how to read me equally well. And she knows that before she can ever get across her point of view, she is wise to ask forgiveness for hurting me. It is in the spirit of mutual forgiveness and a desire for mutual continuation of our relationship in love that conflicts are genuinely resolved, a torn relationship is mended, and difficulties are turned into paving stones for a stronger foundation.

STAGE TWO: A CHANGE OF HEART

When conflict arises, and both parties recognize that something has gone awry in their relationship, someone must experience a change of heart if there is eventually to be a full reconciliation or resolution. That change of heart will then lead a person to "go after" the other mate to make amends and to resolve the conflict.

The bride of Solomon realized quickly that she and Solomon were in conflict and that she erred in her behavior:

> *My heart leaped up when he spoke.*
> *I sought him, but I could not find him;*
> *I called him, but he gave me no answer.*
> *The watchmen who went about the city found me.*
> *They struck me, they wounded me;*
> *The keepers of the walls*
> *Took my veil away from me.*
> *I charge you, O daughters of Jerusalem,*
> *If you find my beloved,*
> *That you tell him I am lovesick!* (Song 5:6–8)

This passage is in sharp contrast to an earlier passage. Read what the same woman said just two chapters earlier:

> *"I will rise now," I said,*
> *"And go about the city;*

In the streets and in the squares
I will seek the one I love."
I sought him, but I did not find him.
The watchmen who go about the city found me;
I said,
"Have you seen the one I love?"
Scarcely had I passed by them,
When I found the one I love. (Song 3:2–4)

When the woman was in close fellowship with God and her fiancé, she looked for her beloved and found him quickly; the watchmen helped her. Now, in this conflict in their marriage, when she acted in selfishness—not God's desirable response for her to have—and she barred her husband from her room, she went out looking for her husband but did not find him. The watchmen did not help her. Rather they struck and wounded her, and shamed her by taking away her veil.

Solomon's wife was faced with a situation in which she knew that she erred, and she felt pain in the conviction of her error. God chastened her.

No matter how you feel the Lord prompting you to respond to a conflict, you should feel remorse that any type of conflict has occurred. You are to lament the fact that the marriage relationship has suffered an injury, regardless of what happened or who was responsible for initiating the conflict. The woman felt the full sting and pain of what she had done.

Solomon did not inflict the pain upon her; it was the "watchmen," the faithful guardians of God's people. If your spouse wrongs you, give God some time to work in your mate's heart. Let God have an opportunity to deal with the conscience of your spouse. Your role is not to have that of the Holy Spirit in your spouse's life. My role as a husband is to teach my wife what I know to be true, love her tenderly, care for her, and provide for her all that she needs, but I am not her Savior, her divine Spirit of truth, or her Comforter and Counselor. Only the Lord can fill those roles.

I have counseled many couples in which either the husband or the wife continually nags the other about what the other does wrong before the Lord. These beleaguered, nagged spouses can't hear the voice of the Lord because the spouse is talking so loudly! They feel manipulated, put upon, and downtrodden. My advice to the nagging spouse is to keep quiet and let God work. It's amazing how God moves into a person's life. Truly His ways *are* higher than man's ways, and His methods are not only very creative but extremely effective!

Early in our marriage, my wife was lying in bed one morning, and I said, "Teresa, get up and fix me some breakfast!" I was teasing her, but my words didn't exactly come out in the teasing way that I meant for them to sound. At the same time I spoke those words, I picked up a metric stick that I owned—a four-sided stick with a steel border on one side—and I cracked that stick down on what I *thought* was a lump in the sheets. It was my wife's leg! I had hit her hard. I saw her eyes puddle up with tears of pain, and I immediately fled to the kitchen in contrition, determined to serve my wife breakfast in bed!

I popped the top off the orange juice container, and in my hurry to make amends for my bad behavior, I poured orange juice down my front. At that point, Teresa walked into the kitchen, and I turned toward her, covered in orange juice, and said, "You prayed for that." She sweetly said, "Come here, Sweetheart," inviting me for a comforting hug, but as I turned toward her, I hit my head on the corner of the cabinet, and suddenly there was blood trickling down from my forehead and mingling with the spilled orange juice. I was a mess.

Did I ever again attempt to tease my wife about fixing my

breakfast, using a metric stick to emphasize my point? No way. For her part, Teresa was kind enough never to bring up the matter again. She knew God had dealt with me in a better way than she ever could have.

There was no manipulation whatsoever in the scene in the Song of Solomon. There was no bargaining—"you do this for me and I'll do that for you." Bargaining results in manipulation, not ministry.

There were no threats, veiled or unveiled. So often I hear of wives who say to their husbands, "If you don't change this . . ." or "If you don't do such and so for me, I'm going to leave you." In their heart of hearts they have no intent of leaving their husbands. They are threatening something they never intend to do. It's wrong to threaten abandonment, separation, or divorce in order to get your way in a marriage. That's manipulation, not ministry.

A woman asked me after I had presented the information in this chapter, "If I can't leave him, can I kill him?" No, you can't do that either!

But you can continue to love your spouse and to pray for your spouse. Ask God to do what you cannot do, and that is to change the human heart and transform the human mind.

State what you feel you must state, make whatever requests you believe are right to make, put forth your case as best you can make it, but don't attempt to force a change in your mate. Leave that up to God.

I heard a priceless story about this subject. A woman asked her husband one morning to zip up the back of her dress. He began to play around with the zipper in a flirtatious way—zipping it up and down, up and down—and in the process, the zipper broke. She had just had the dress dry-cleaned and was late for a meeting, and there she stood with a "broken" dress. She was furious.

About 5:30 that evening, she returned home, still angry over her husband's behavior that morning. She found her husband working on his car, lying underneath the car from his waist up, the lower part of his body sticking out and temptingly accessible. He didn't seem to hear her as she approached, so she reached down and grabbed the zipper on the front of his jeans and began to zip it up and down just as he had done with her dress that morning. Then she walked into the house.

To her astonishment, her husband was standing in the kitchen. She said, "What are you doing in here?" He said, "What do you mean? It's our kitchen."

She said, "You were under the car just two seconds ago."

"No," he said, "I haven't been under the car at all."

"Well, who is out there in our garage working under your car?"

"It's the next-door neighbor," he said. "The muffler was coming off and he volunteered to fix it, so I told him I'd really appreciate his help and I came in here to fix a glass of tea for him when he's finished."

His wife went pale as a white sheet. She admitted to her husband what she had done, and they both hurried out to apologize to the man. They found the guy lying totally still. He didn't respond to their calls, so they pulled him out from under the car by his legs. When he came to, they discovered that he had done what any man would have done if someone suddenly grabbed the zipper to his pants. He sat straight up, and bam, he hit his head on the underside of the car with such force that he knocked himself out!

All acts of revenge need to be left to God. Strange and terrible things can happen when you take retaliation and vengeance into your hands, and none of them are good.

One of the most effective responses I've ever heard given to a husband who erred in his behavior was one that a wife gave after hearing a sermon about Jesus and Pilate. Pilate said to Jesus, "Do You not know that I have power to crucify You, and power to release You?" Jesus replied, "You could have no power at all against Me unless it had been given you from above" (John 19:10–11). From that moment on, Pilate sought to find a way to release Jesus because he recognized that he, indeed, was under God's authority.

This young woman said to me, "When my husband makes a decision or embarks on an activity that I know is wrong, I just say to him, 'Do what you want. You are under God's authority, and I trust God to deal with you.'" That's called submission with a wallop to it! The truth remains, however. All of us are under the authority of someone, and in the marriage chain of command, a husband is under the authority of God. A wife is wise to trust God to manifest His authority in her husband's life rather than to attempt to take on that role for herself.

How did the bride's heart change once she realized her error? Surely God was at work in her, for no act of man could bring about such a complete and quick change of heart. At one moment she was angry with Solomon for awakening her and she selfishly rejected him. Just a short time later, she was fearful that she might lose her husband and was ardent in her desire for him:

> *What is your beloved*
> *More than another beloved,*
> *O fairest among women?*
> *What is your beloved*
> *More than another beloved,*
> *That you so charge us?* (Song 5:9)

The woman began to dwell on all of the wonderful aspects of her husband, those things that set him apart from other men and made him so special to her. She thought about all her reasons for loving him and for giving to him generously rather than withholding from him in selfishness. She now saw her sin in the light of his goodness:

My beloved is white and ruddy,
Chief among ten thousand.
His head is like the finest gold;
His locks are wavy,
And black as a raven.
His eyes are like doves
By the rivers of waters,
Washed with milk,
And fitly set.
His cheeks are like a bed of spices,
Banks of scented herbs.
His lips are lilies,
Dripping liquid myrrh.
His hands are rods of gold
Set with beryl.
His body is carved ivory
Inlaid with sapphires.
His legs are pillars of marble
Set on bases of fine gold.
His countenance is like Lebanon,
Excellent as the cedars.
His mouth is most sweet,
Yes, he is altogether lovely.
This is my beloved,
And this is my friend,
O daughters of Jerusalem! (Song 5:10–16)

These are some of Solomon's features that his wife called to her mind and praised:

- He was pure in his motives and behaviors toward her. Repeatedly she referred to him as white, including white as ivory and white as marble.

- He was extremely handsome—more handsome even than ten thousand other men combined.

- His head (in this case his mind) was filled with wisdom more valuable than gold.

- He was respected even though he was youthful. His hair was black, with no evidence of the weakness of age. Sin is often pictured in the Bible as the weakness of aging. (See Hos. 7:9.)

- He was gentle; his eyes were soft and tender toward her.

- He was sober. The whites of his eyes were white, not reddened by alcohol or debauched living.

- He had a steadfast gaze and clear outlook toward her. His eyes were "fitly set," which means they were wide open and focused on her. He saw her, and her alone, among all other women. It is also a reference to the fact that Solomon did not have a shifty look to his eyes; his eyes did not narrow in anger or mistrust, they never openly flared in anger, and they were never bored into dullness. They were eyes of immutable kindness and unchanging blessing toward her.

- He was compassionate toward her. When he held her in his arms, cheek to cheek, there was a sweetness in his expression of love. When he kissed her, he did so tenderly and sweetly. He dealt with her in a forgiving, tender, romantic, and loving way at all times.

- He was strong in authority. A king's position was often revealed by the wide jeweled bands of gold that he wore on each arm, a sign of his strength in leadership over a nation, people, or empire. Solomon had great bearing in his role as king. He was a "manly man" to his wife, strong in leadership and authority in their relationship. That in no way left room for abuse. I have counseled women who have come to me with bruises on their arms and faces. I want to amputate the arms of the men who have hurt them! Solomon was strong in authority, but he was never a bully. He led by example, not by demand.

- He was spiritually strong. Strength of spirit was—and continues to be—associated with strength in the abdominal area. The "belly" area has long been considered by the Jewish people to be the locus of one's eternal spirit. Solomon exerted spiritual leadership in their home. He was like a strong rock, a marble statue that could not be moved readily. Furthermore, the statue was set on a base of gold. Solomon's character was established on eternal things of utmost value. In the eyes of his wife, Solomon was grounded on the Word of God, and he could not be moved from his position before the Lord.
- He was physically strong. Physical strength is repeatedly associated with a person's legs and the ability to stand strong in the face of assault, battle, or calamity.
- He stood tall on the inside as well as the outside, just as the cedars of Lebanon grew to great heights and were among the noblest of trees. Solomon had a bearing about him of self-confidence and self-esteem because he knew who he was in God's eyes.
- His words were spoken with kindness—his mouth was a source of sweetness toward her.

She concluded, "He is altogether lovely. He is everything I want in a husband." God truly changed her heart, as her husband was kind in the face of wrong. In the light of her newly awakened awareness of all the good qualities in her husband, she had a strong desire to be the wife he longed to have.

The woman is a fine example of what God does in transforming a person's attitude. First, she begins to see things in a new light. She begins to see the good that has escaped her before. *She sees her mate as God sees her mate!* When that happens, compassion rises in her heart. And in the wake of compassion, she feels a desire for renewed intimacy and closeness of communication.

STAGE THREE: REACHING OUT TO MAKE AMENDS

Once Solomon's wife renewed within her mind a right attitude and a loving perspective toward her husband, she went in search of Solomon. That's why the daughters of Jerusalem asked,

> *Where has your beloved gone,*
> *O fairest among women?*
> *Where has your beloved turned aside,*
> *That we may seek him with you?* (Song 6:1)

She had a desire to find Solomon and to make things right. At that point, others were not perceived as hindering her, shaming her, or hurting her; rather, they were volunteering to help her. Her conscience was clear. Her instincts were alive and functioning toward reconciliation. God was again working with her to find and recover what she had rejected.

The good news for the wife was that she knew exactly where her husband was to be found. Why? Because he had an unchanging character. He was not one person on one day, and another person in temperament, personality, and conviction on the next day. He was consistent in his beliefs, his ethics, his morality, his attitudes, his opinions, his behavior. He could be counted on to be who he was and to stand for all the things he considered to be important. She said,

> *My beloved has gone to his garden,*
> *To the beds of spices,*
> *To feed his flock in the gardens,*
> *And to gather lilies.* (Song 6:2)

Solomon was going about the work and routine of his life. He was doing important work—cultivating the beds of spices that were vital both to the preservation and to the appeal of food. This could mean that Solomon, as king, was doing what was important to maintain his empire and to make it appealing to its citizens and to those who might seek refuge in it. He exhibited the same qualities to his wife, cultivating what was good for the preservation of their home, doing what it took to keep himself appealing to his wife.

Solomon was also continuing to take the role of a good shepherd—one who would defend his flock just as he defended her and their home, one who would lead his flock into pastures and to pure sources of water—providing for his flock just as he provided for her. Solomon was about the work of defending his kingdom and home. He continued to do all he could to provide for his family.

Solomon was also gathering the fair lilies. In other words, he was a blessing to others in his endeavors, and he was causing others who were weaker and more fragile to delight in his strength and tender care of them.

The point of greatest assurance for Solomon's wife was this: "I am my beloved's, and my beloved is mine. He feeds his flock among the lilies" (Song 6:3). She had absolutely no doubts about his commitment to her or her commitment to him. Regardless of the conflict they had—their spat, their argument, their difference of opinion, their momentary display of bad behavior—they were committed to having an "us" relationship. They were one.

What a wonderful thing for a wife to know that her husband bears these qualities that Solomon's wife attributes to Solomon! Show me a wife who knows that her husband is doing all that he can do, with an unfailing commitment to their marriage, and I will show you a happily married woman.

In like manner, it is a great joy to a man to know that while he is at work each day, his wife is doing all that she can to preserve and enrich their marriage, to protect and provide for their children and home, and to do so with a gentle and quiet spirit, and all with an unfailing commitment to be faithful to him. Such a man has absolute trust in his wife and takes refuge in her company.

Solomon's bride was reaching out to him with love and appreciation. She was prepared to make whatever amends were necessary to maintain their relationship: "I am his and he is mine."

Many things can be done in virtually every marriage to bring about reconciliation, but the bottom line of all of them is this: a desire to see the relationship reconciled and restored to a deep level of love. Unless there is a desire to reconcile, no reconciliation can occur. If both parties have a deep desire to reconcile, reconciliation is nearly always possible.

Sometimes one spouse will need to abandon "rights" in order to renew or restore the relationship. Each spouse must recognize that individual rights within a marriage are never more important than the unity and love of the relationship as a whole. If in demanding your rights or insisting that you have the right idea or opinion, you are threatening to destroy the harmony and loving foundation of your home, you are wrong, no matter how right you think you are. A greater harm is in danger of being done to your marriage and your family by your stubborn resistance than ever could have been done to you personally in the first place.

There may be cases in which one person needs to separate momentarily from a spouse who is abusive, out of control, suffering from an addiction, or in need of physical or emotional treatment. But in such cases where separation may be necessary, the spouse who leaves can leave the marriage physically and still not leave it emotionally or spiritually. The spouse can continue to trust God, believe for God's best, and hold out hope for healing and reconciliation.

If one spouse insists upon personal rights and a total abdication of all rights by the other person—in other words, if one person continues to insist that he is 100 percent right, the other person is 100 percent wrong, and one spouse needs to be in total subjection to the other—a marriage is inevitably in serious trouble. The boat has been rocked so severely to one side that it will fill with water and capsize.

The bride *went after* Solomon, seeking to make amends. She went in a spirit of appreciation for him, contrition in her heart, and a desire for reconciliation. That's the attitude one must have if conflict is to be resolved.

Had she stayed at home, waiting for Solomon to come to his senses and make another attempt at being with her, her story might have had a very different ending.

Once she was in his presence, what did she do? How was the conflict resolved? We'll deal with *conflict resolution* in the next chapter.

Questions to Think About or Discuss

1. *Can you and your beloved fight "clean and fair"?*
2. *How difficult is it for you to respond with love after you have been hurt? From where do you draw your strength and courage not to retaliate or seek revenge?*
3. *What are the traits in your beloved that you have come to appreciate even more as the result of experiencing conflicts in your relationship?*

Seven

The Resolution of Conflict

Song of Solomon 6:4–13

Marital disagreements, arguments, and conflicts are inevitable.

Why?

Because marriage vows do not erase differences in individual personalities, opinions, ideas, and past histories. No matter how much of a union a couple may achieve physically, socially, sexually, materially, and spiritually, each spouse continues to maintain a unique personality. Each spouse continues to have an identity, a degree of self-esteem, and specific gifts and talents that flow from God and are intended to be used for God's purposes.

When two people marry, their individual identities do not disappear. Rather, their two identities blend together to create a greater, richer, and more wonderful whole. This blending of differences into a unique and appealing new entity requires that some parts of each individual be sanded away or refined so that the two people might complement each other in all ways and so that their home might function with efficiency and be overflowing in Christian ministry.

Conflict is inevitable; resolution is not. It is to be highly desired, sought after, and prayed for. It is something to be set as a goal any time conflict arises. Resolution is not automatic. It doesn't happen over time or by accident. For a conflict to be resolved, there must be an intentional desire for reconciliation followed by reconciliatory acts. Resolution requires effort, time, and a certain degree of skill.

Conflicts often happen through carelessness; they occur by accident. Resolution takes place when both persons care enough to work hard to achieve it. Resolution occurs on purpose.

In the last chapter, we covered the first three stages in marital conflicts and their resolution:

1. A feeling of harm, hurt, or injury on the part of both persons.
2. A change of heart on the part of the one who initiated the conflict.
3. A desire on the part of both persons for the conflict to end.

Each of these first three stages deals primarily with conflict—an awareness of the conflict, a response to the conflict, and a desire in the heart to resolve the conflict. In this chapter, we will focus on what the couple did to bring about resolution.

STAGE FOUR: COMMUNICATION

Most marriage conflicts tend to arise from one of five sources: (1) a failure of communication, (2) financial difficulties, (3) sexual difficulties, (4) problems with in-laws, or (5) disagreements about child rearing. Furthermore, marital conflicts pretty much occur in this descending order. A failure in communication or, perhaps better stated, poor communication accounts for the majority of the problems I see as a pastoral counselor.

For resolution to occur, good, satisfying communication must take place between the two people in conflict. That happened in the Song of Solomon. As soon as Solomon's bride found Solomon, communication took place. They did not stand and stare at each other in silence. They did not tiptoe around each other, looking for something to say to break the ice. Solomon spoke to his bride. What he had to say to his bride was extremely important, but we'll deal with that a little later. For now, the main point I want to convey is that communication is vital to a good marriage. A conflict does not resolve itself in silence—the conflict simply goes underground, just under the surface of behavior in the relationship, where it will fester and continue to be a source of irritation in the heart of one or both spouses.

In the premarital counseling sessions that I conduct with engaged couples, I look very closely at the way the two people relate to each other in my office. It's amazing what I can tell by watching and listening. I can tell if one or both of them are uncomfortable discussing a certain topic, if one dominates the conversation (and very likely the relationship), or if one or both are quick to display anger or a defensive attitude, or to fall silent in a pout. If such communication problems are evident at this stage of a relationship, I can guarantee they will extend beyond the wedding vows into marriage. I advise the couple to work more on their communication before they proceed with their wedding plans.

Let me share with you the sixteen axiomatic "nevers" that I believe are integral for good communication between spouses when conflict occurs.

1. Never Speak Rashly

Weigh your words before you speak, especially if you are feeling emotionally upset about a situation or circumstance. Back away and give your endocrine system a chance to return to normal. Always keep in mind that it's not only what you say that matters, but how and when you speak.

Proverbs 27:14 offers this admonition: "He who blesses his friend with a loud voice, rising early in the morning, it will be counted a curse to him." This blessing actually refers to a shout that awakens and disturbs a friend. The person who does that will not have his day go well, for the "friend" will surely seek retaliation. In other words, it's great to call out a friendly hello to a friend, just not at 5:00 A.M. directly below his bedroom window.

Very often in a marriage, a person reacts to *how* a person speaks far more than to what is said. An angry, belittling, or hateful tone of voice is going to bring about a response, even if *what* is said is rather benign. The more benign the content of such communication, the more the statement is going to be perceived as sarcasm or cynicism, which also brings about a negative response in most people. Proverbs 15:1 tells us, "A harsh word stirs up anger."

2. Never Confront Your Mate Publicly

Have you ever watched or overheard a couple argue in a public place, perhaps at the table next to you in a restaurant? You feel sorry for both persons—the one who is the recipient of an angry harangue and the one who is engaging in such terrible behavior because that person doesn't realize how much embarrassment he is bringing upon himself. Jesus taught, "If your brother sins against you, go and tell him his fault between you and him alone" (Matt. 18:15).

If you have an issue to bring up with your spouse, do so in the privacy of your home.

3. Never Confront Your Spouse in Your Children's Presence

Your children in no way benefit from watching the two of you quarrel. They will invariably respond more to the tone of your disagreement than to what is being said. They will feel defensive for themselves and defensive for the spouse they feel is getting a verbal lashing. They are likely to disrespect both parents for engaging in this behavior, either at the time or in later years. As a parent, you have the job of modeling good communication before your children. Heated arguments or confrontational, combative, critical statements are *not* good communication for children to copy. Proverbs 17:1 affirms, "Better is a dry morsel with quietness, than a house full of feasting with strife." A tense home will make a boy long for his driver's license so he can be free of it. A young girl will long for some man to remove her from it—all too often, the wrong man.

4. Never Use Your Children in the Conflict

Sometimes parents ask one of their children to side with them in an argument, to help them in their defense, or even to lie for them. Again, this is not modeling good communication skills or good conflict resolution. A child needs the assurance that both parents love each other and are able to resolve their differences by themselves. To ask a child to side with one parent is to put the child in an extremely awkward and undesirable position.

Too many people I know have been pulled between their parents like a rope in a tug-of-war match. They resent the fact that their parents did that to them and they feel less respect for both parents as a result.

5. Never Say "Never" or "Always"

The tendency in a conflict is to take an issue to the extreme: "You *always* do this," or "You *never* do that." Very few things in life happen in *never* or *always* terms. It's far more productive to say, "I don't appreciate it when . . ." or "I feel bad when you . . ." and then state the specific behavior. Don't generalize or use broad terms. Be specific in citing behavior.

Never and *always* are terms that polarize and define a person. Stay neutral in your emotions. Don't push your argument, or your spouse, to an extreme position.

6. Never Resort to Name-Calling

Name-calling in an argument is a form of generalization, which is never productive or accurate. Name-calling is always negative in tone and negative in effect. A name-caller cites a weakness or flaw in the other person and exaggerates it. The way to resolution in conflict is to become specific and to take the heat and hurt out of one's spoken words. Name-calling is a surefire way to turn up both the heat and the hurt in an argument.

7. Never Get Historical

You may be thinking, *Don't you mean hysterical, Tommy?* No, historical. Don't dredge up the past. In recalling past sins and applying them to the most recent bad behavior or error, you are sending a strong signal to your spouse that you are *not* a forgiving person. A truly forgiving person endeavors not only to forgive, but also to forget. Although you may not ever truly be able to forget an incident, you can forget to bring it up. I'm always amazed when a person can recall in a counseling session, "Don't you remember five years ago when you . . . ?" Such statements tell me that the person who is making them is bitter and angry at a very deep level. The bitterness and anger are far more important to address than any act of misbehavior, error, or sin committed five years ago.

8. Never Stomp Out of the Room or Leave

This is a form of domination, a form of gaining victory, and it will produce nothing but unresolved and heightened anger.

9. Never Raise Your Voice in Anger

Anger turns any statement into a sin and any discussion into an unresolved debate. It is a primitive form of winning the argument. If anger creeps into a conversation or discussion, the anger must first be addressed, defused, and forgiven before any other issue can be dealt with. Proverbs 16:21 asserts, "Sweetness of the lips increases learning," and Proverbs 16:24 adds, "Pleasant words are like a honeycomb, sweetness to the soul and health to the bones." A quiet, sweet tone of voice makes a person much more persuasive and brings about a much better attitude in the person who is listening.

10. Never Bring Family Members into the Discussion Unless They Are a Direct Part of the Problem Being Addressed

In other words, never say to a person, "You are just like your father," or "Your mother does this and it drives me nuts, and now you're doing it too." Regardless of the accuracy of your statement, your spouse is going to be defensive about his or her parents. Very little can be accomplished in a discussion if parents or in-laws are brought into the discussion because they will then become the focal point of the argument.

11. Never Win Through Reasoning or Logic and Never Out-Argue

Arguments are fueled by a competitive spirit that insists upon winning. Conflicts are resolved when one person chooses willfully to "lose" or to abandon a position and yield to the other person. Nothing is more disrespectful than to disregard the feelings of your mate with cold logic as if your mate's pain is foolish and imagined.

Is this a doormat position? No. To the contrary. It is a godly position. Repeatedly through the New Testament we find admonitions that we are to submit to other believers.

Rather than to defend a position of personal "right," we are to submit our personal rights to a greater position of seeking unity and harmony within the body of Christ.

When you win a conflict, and do so repeatedly, you are likely to lose a mate. Press to resolve, but not to achieve victory.

Resolution means that both persons come to a position where they feel that their feelings and ideas have been expressed, understood, and valued, and then a decision is made that accommodates as best as possible the feelings and ideas of both persons. There are no winners or losers. Rather, there is the advancement of the relationship to a new level of understanding and agreement, usually with compromise by both persons.

This is not to say that we are to compromise with evil. If a spouse is intent on engaging in evil behavior that involves both spouses or the family as a whole, there is no way that the other spouse should contribute to or accommodate that behavior. Seek every means possible of convincing your spouse that what he is about to do is unrighteous before God and dangerous to the integrity of your marriage and family. Make every appeal you can make to the person to turn away from evil and toward the things of God. Pray diligently and fervently that God will drop the scales of deceit from your spouse's eyes so that he might see clearly the full ramifications of what is being done and come to himself, and in the process, repent of his ungodly behavior. If you continually win arguments your mate will lose heart, go silent, and emotionally withdraw.

12. Never Be Condescending

Arguments are rarely resolved if one person adopts a "know it all" or "better than thou" attitude. If condescending behavior is manifested in a public setting, the spouse who is being talked down to is likely to be angry and embarrassed.

Whether you are husband or wife, your role in marriage is to build up, to edify, to strengthen, and to genuinely praise the goodness of God in your spouse. A condescending attitude does just the opposite—it tears down a person and weakens him in his own eyes and in the eyes of others.

13. Never Demean

Some people don't condescend in tone; they demean in actual content of their communication. There was nothing at all condescending about the tone of one man who sat in my pastoral counseling office as he said very matter-of-factly, "My wife isn't well educated and doesn't know about these things." He had no idea that he was hurting his wife in making a statement like that. He could hardly fathom the fact that she was embarrassed and upset by his remark, which he perceived to be a simple fact. He even said to me, "I'm telling the truth, and if the truth hurts a little, so be it. You've got to face the truth."

Much truth in our world never needs to be said. And there is no greater truth than this: we are to love one another at all times. If telling the truth to a person clashes with expressing love to that person, err on the side of expressing love. There is no excuse at any time for demeaning a person. Rather, focus on all of the good qualities and traits that God has put into your spouse. Build up these attributes. Praise the good. You may be amazed to see how the bad pales into the background of your relationship.

A tone of voice can also be demeaning if it causes another person to feel humiliation or embarrassment. I was in a conversation with a man and his wife. For no apparent reason, the wife dropped her eyeglasses as we talked. Then a few minutes after she had picked them up, she dropped them again. At that point, her husband turned to her and said in an extremely demeaning tone of voice, "Put those glasses on your face and keep 'em there, or I'm gonna break 'em!" I watched her shrivel emotionally in our presence. I wanted to do my own lashing out at him. He was acting like a bully, and in the end, he was demeaning himself by making such remarks about his wife.

14. Never Accuse Your Spouse with "You" Statements

Arguments escalate when you continually point to the other person and say such things as, "You did this," "You said that," "You caused this," or "You are a rotten person." You have taken on the roles of both judge and jury. Instead, couch your statements in "I" terms: "I heard this and I need to know if I heard you correctly," "I don't understand what you mean when you say . . . ," or "I felt this way when I heard what you said."

15. Never Allow an Argument to Begin If Both of You Are Overly Tired, If One of You Is Under the Influence of Chemicals, or If One of You Is Physically Ill

Abigail, the wife of a foolish man named Nabal, had the good sense not to tell her husband what a grievous error he had made until he was sober enough to hear her fully. (See 1 Sam. 25.) A person who is physically ill, is under the influence of alcohol, drugs, or heavy-duty prescription medications, or is exhausted physically or emotionally cannot engage in a reasonable, logical, rational conversation. If your spouse lashes out at you while he or she is drunk, extremely tired, or ill, wait until the context changes before you respond or bring up an issue for discussion. One noted speaker on marriage has given this advice: never start an argument after ten o'clock at night.

16. Never Touch Your Spouse in a Harmful Manner

No grabbing, no slapping, no shaking, no pushing, no strong-arming. Rough physical treatment is never justifiable.

LISTENING IS JUST AS IMPORTANT AS SPEAKING

Each of the statements of advice just given relates to what a person should and should not *say* or *do* in times of conflict. It is equally important that a person know how to *listen* in times of conflict. There are times when silence is even more important than speaking. Let me share with you five pieces of advice about listening.

1. Listen with Patience Until Your Spouse Speaks

Don't force a quiet mate to talk. Sometimes a person needs time to digest an experience or a statement. Don't force your spouse to respond immediately to what you say.

2. Listen with Your Face

Men have the ability to listen and do other things at the same time. Their wives do *not* find this the least bit satisfying. A woman wants to feel that she has her husband's undivided attention. Look at your wife when she speaks. Look into her eyes. Give her your full attention.

My wife, Teresa, taught me this. One day when she was talking to me and she perceived that I was not paying close enough attention to her, she pulled my face around to hers so that we were looking at each other eyeball-to-eyeball, and she said, "Listen to me with your face, Tommy." I did, and I do. Often a woman needs only to express her heart. She doesn't need answers or a logical evaluation, only consideration.

3. Listen Until Your Spouse Has Finished Speaking

Don't interrupt, and don't hem and haw while your spouse is speaking. Husband, if your wife wants to talk about something that you don't care to talk about, choose to talk about the matter anyway. It may seem unimportant or trivial to you, but it isn't unimportant or trivial to her. Give her the respect of hearing her out on whatever topic she feels a need to vent or voice an opinion. Proverbs 18:13 offers good advice: "He who answers a matter before he hears it, it is folly and shame to him."

A very upset woman called me one day. She and her husband had had a verbal disagreement, and he had walked out on her while she was talking. He just stomped off in anger, not wanting to hear what she had to say. She was angry, hurt, and a little fearful that he might never return. He did, of course, acting as if nothing had occurred between them. That only confused and hurt her all the more.

The next time I saw the man in a counseling situation, I said, "Don't ever do that again." He tried to shrug off the incident as unimportant. I said, "This is not a minor problem. It's a potential cancer eating away at your relationship. Stay in the room and hear what your wife has to say. Don't walk out. She may have some valuable information to share with you that can be of benefit to you, not only in your marriage but in your other relationships. And even if what she shares with you isn't all that beneficial or important, you will at least have heard all that she has to say so that you are mulling over her *full* message when you reflect on the matter later." Remember, every person deems his or her opinion to be important.

4. Listen and Then File Away What You Hear in the Closet of Privacy

What is said in times of marital conflict should be said in privacy and kept in privacy. Don't vent your spleen to others outside your marriage. Women, don't go to the other women in the beauty shop and talk about your "worthless mate." Guys, don't escape to the club and talk about your "sorry wife." Don't try to drum up support for your position in an argument outside your marriage. Two things will result. First, those to whom you speak will think less of your spouse and, ultimately, less of you for talking about your spouse. Second, when you share private matters related to your marriage with others outside your marriage, you damage the trust level of your spouse.

The only "outside" person to whom you may talk about conflicts in your marriage should be a professional counselor—Christian psychologist or pastoral counselor—who will keep all that you say in strictest confidence. All others should be kept out of the arena of your arguments or disagreements, especially parents who will probably wreak judgment on the one who has harmed their darling.

5. Listen Without Rude Body Language

Some spouses say, "Okay, I'll sit down and listen to you," but everything about their body language and facial gestures indicates, "I think this is a waste of time and there's no reason for this," or "I won't give anything you say much weight, and I may not even believe you." Smirks, facial grimaces, turned shoulders, and aggressive stares are all acts that fuel a conflict rather than defuse it.

Choose to listen to your mate with a mind open to learning and growing. Listen with your whole heart. Listen with a sincere intent to communicate fully and to bring a matter to reconciliation.

How you listen and how you greet a spouse the next time you encounter your mate after a disagreement will greatly determine whether a conflict ends quickly or extends over time.

STAGE FIVE: FORGIVENESS

Much can happen in a very short period if one person will make a positive move toward breaking an icy silence or cooling off a heated discussion.

The Resolution of Conflict

In the conflict between Solomon and his bride, we might have written one of these two scenarios as the next phase:

1. The bride came very apologetically to her husband, he stood in silence until she apologized fully, and then he forgave her.
2. The bride came to him and before she could say anything, the husband lashed out at her for what she had done wrong. In her repentant frame of mind, she took his scolding in silence and then asked for forgiveness, which he granted.

The Song of Solomon, however, presents a very different approach. We have a wonderful example of how God desires for us to reconcile our differences and to deal with a spouse who has hurt us. Solomon greeted his spouse by saying,

> *O my love, you are as beautiful as Tirzah,*
> *Lovely as Jerusalem,*
> *Awesome as an army with banners!*
> *Turn your eyes away from me,*
> *For they have overcome me.*
> *Your hair is like a flock of goats*
> *Going down from Gilead.*
> *Your teeth are like a flock of sheep*
> *Which have come up from the washing;*
> *Every one bears twins,*
> *And none is barren among them.*
> *Like a piece of pomegranate*
> *Are your temples behind your veil.* (Song 6:4–7)

Rather than displaying silence in expectation of an apology or an angry response, Solomon greeted his bride with genuine compliments, telling her essentially, "You are as lovely as I remember you on our wedding night, and I respect you fully as my wife. You are my delight [which is the literal meaning of the word *Tirzah*] and my soul's refuge of peace [which is the literal meaning of *Jerusalem*]. I feel the same excitement in your presence as I have always felt, just as much excitement as a kid watching a parade with banners and pageantry!"

Solomon spoke to his wife in the same terms that he used on their wedding night, noting very specific aspects of her beauty—her eyes, her smile, her blush. She was so beautiful that he stated he could not concentrate on what he was saying. He asked her to turn away her eyes because they confused him. What reinforcement! He concluded,

> *There are sixty queens*
> *And eighty concubines,*
> *And virgins without number.*
> *My dove, my perfect one,*
> *Is the only one,*
> *The only one of her mother,*
> *The favorite of the one who bore her.*
> *The daughters saw her*
> *And called her blessed,*
> *The queens and the concubines,*
> *And they praised her.*
> *Who is she who looks forth as the morning,*
> *Fair as the moon,*
> *Clear as the sun,*
> *Awesome as an army with banners?* (Song 6:8–10)

In a nutshell, Solomon was conveying to his bride that in his eyes, she was the only woman in the world who mattered to him. She was one of a kind in his love. She had no equal.

What was Solomon doing? He was forgiving his bride *even before she had a chance to ask for forgiveness.* He was granting her a full reconciliation and a full pardon for any offense she might have committed against him.

She was already feeling repentant, but Solomon didn't know that. He forgave her out of the generosity of his heart. He freely forgave, without demanding an apology or penance for her misdeeds. His bride no doubt fully accepted the generous outpouring of forgiveness and was grateful for it.

Nothing brings about reconciliation quicker in a relationship than these two elements: (1) a repentant heart on the part of the person who has wronged another, and (2) a heart overflowing with unconditional love and forgiveness on the part of the person who has been wronged.

In any conflict, each spouse is wise to have a repentant and a forgiving heart. You likely have been partly wrong—be fully repentant. And then, be fully forgiving for whatever wrong your mate has committed against you. A couple who adopts this stance toward conflict will have a marriage in which conflicts are likely to be very brief and quickly healed. Each spouse must determine in his or her own heart, "When conflicts arise, I will choose not to hurt my mate, but if any hurt results, I will take responsibility for that hurt, I will repent for causing hurt, and I will fully forgive my spouse for any wrong done to me."

Solomon took this stance toward his bride: "I can't even remember what you did." He forgave in such a way that he chose not to file away the incident in his memory bank so that he might bring it up at a later time. He put the incident behind him and was facing toward their future.

I have met couples who seem to pick at a situation over and over, almost like vultures on a carcass. They remind each other of past hurts, mistakes, and even foibles as if desiring to keep alive a painful insult or incident. Let such things go!

If you forgive, then forgive fully. Don't bring up the hurtful incident in the future. Move on with your lives.

"Isn't this sweeping an issue under the rug?" you may ask.

No, it's bringing a hurtful situation to its death and burying it. This is not denial or a Pollyanna attitude toward pain. It is *forgiveness,* which is very active, very intentional, very positive, and very courageous.

Clara Barton, the founder of the Red Cross in the United States, was once asked about a negative incident in her life in which Clara had been hurt. She responded to her questioner, "I distinctly remember forgetting that." What an important attitude to have in extending forgiveness.

Genuine forgiveness must be freely and fully granted. It is an act of unwarranted, generous mercy. Solomon's bride received such forgiveness:

> *I went down to the garden of nuts*
> *To see the verdure of the valley,*
> *To see whether the vine had budded*
> *And the pomegranates had bloomed.*
> *Before I was even aware,*
> *My soul had made me*
> *As the chariots of my noble people.* (Song 6:11–12)

She said, "I went to find out if there was still hope for fruitfulness in our relationship, and before I knew it, my soul—my love, my husband, Solomon—had fully forgiven me!"

In the Hebrew culture, one of the highest forms of recognition and reconciliation that could be granted to another person was to ask that person to ride with you in your chariot. It was a sign of total trust as well as a public display of relationship between the two of you. We have an example in the Bible when Ahab, the king of Israel, was condemned by God for allowing a Syrian enemy to ride in his chariot with him. Ahab's act indicated that he was in league with the Syrians, that they were one in purpose, and that they had formed an alliance. (See 1 Kings 20:33.)

When Solomon's bride gave reference to chariots, she was stating that she knew she had been fully restored to the heart of her husband and furthermore, that her relationship with her husband was strong, for chariots were a picture of might. She experienced full confidence that she had the love of her husband and that they were at peace.

That's what forgiveness does in any relationship, especially in the aftermath of conflict. It restores confidence to both persons that the marriage is strong enough to endure conflict, and it brings about genuine peace in the hearts of both mates. True reconciliation is marked by an atmosphere of rest and comfort—not a stiff, stilted, or uncomfortable silence, but genuine freedom and peace.

STAGE SIX: GREATER CLOSENESS AND JOY

The final stage of conflict resolution is one of greater closeness and joy between the two spouses. Have you ever heard someone say, "Fighting is bad, but making up makes it all worth it"? There is some truth to that statement. We read in the Song of Solomon:

> *Return, return, O Shulamite;*
> *Return, return, that we may look upon you!*
> *What would you see in the Shulamite—*
> *As it were, the dance of the two camps?* (Song 6:13)

"Shulamite" was the nickname for the bride. It was a take-off on the name of Solomon, which in Hebrew is *Shlomo,* a word related to *shalom,* the word for peace and wholeness. It would be as if someone called my wife "Tomasina"—the diminutive or feminine of Tom. Calling the bride the Shulamite was a way of saying, "She is one with Solomon." They were *close*—so close that they couldn't be separated. She was part of him.

What about "the dance of the two camps"? When a couple experience genuine forgiveness in the aftermath of conflict, they are drawn even more tightly or closely together. Solomon and his bride experienced an even greater intimacy and joy in the aftermath of conflict—they rejoiced as if they were having a private party, a dance.

Paul wrote to the Romans, "Where sin abounded, grace abounded much more" (Rom. 5:20). Let that be the truth of your marriage any time a conflict arises. Choose to forgive with a generosity that far exceeds the wrong that has been done to you. Choose to be repentant to a degree far greater than the wrong you have done. Let your coming together in an atmosphere of forgiveness result in a mutuality of joy and a greater warmth and intimacy in your love.

Conflict will arise. Resolution can be achieved. And if done with free-flowing forgiveness and unconditional love as the central features of reconciliation, the resolution of a conflict can result in a marriage that is stronger and more vibrant than before the conflict arose. In many ways, a strong marriage is the result of repeated, healthy conflict resolutions over time.

Don't be discouraged or fearful when conflicts arise. Use them as building stones toward an even more wonderful marriage relationship. On the heels of this conflict and resolution we will see marriage at its most intimate.

Questions to Think About or Discuss

1. *Are you and your beloved able to achieve satisfying resolutions to the conflicts that arise between you?*

2. *Do the arguments between you and your beloved have a winner and a loser?*

3. *What wrongs do you find difficult to forgive or forget?*

4. *In what areas do you need to improve your communication—both listening and speaking?*

Eight

Moving to Deeper Levels

Song of Solomon 7:1–8:4

My wife, Teresa, and I enjoy watching other couples when we go out to eat at restaurants. We can nearly always pick out those who are newlyweds or who are in the stages of dating or courtship. The couples treat each other with tenderness and affection. The man pulls out the chair for the woman; the two of them hold hands across the dinner table; they seem almost oblivious to their food and, at times, to their waiter. The "old marrieds," in comparison, often sit in silence, staring off in space, chewing as quickly as they can to get the meal over with. So often marriage partners start out sizzling with passion and then dissipate into mere roommates.

A loss of romance does not need to occur, yet in so many marriages, it does. The heat of passion and all displays of tender giving seem to vanish, and we accept it as normal, saying, "That's just the way it is."

You perhaps have heard the old story that in the first year of marriage, if the wife gets a cold, the husband nearly smothers her with attention, cold medications, blankets, and concern. By the third year, if the wife gets a cold, the husband goes to the local pharmacy on her behalf, tosses her a bottle of pills as she lies on her sickbed, and leaves her to heal on her own. By the fifth year, if the wife is ill, the husband complains that she isn't covering her mouth when she coughs.

In too many marriages, time seems to erode away, slowly but surely, communication, caring, affection, sensitivity, intimacy, and spontaneity. The marriage begins to revolve more around the children than around the two spouses. When the children leave home, the two then look at each other across the kitchen table and ask, "Who are you?" They've lost the core of what made them a couple in the first place. The two may look back and question what happened. After all, nothing of a serious or prolonged conflict seemed to have occurred. There were no times when divorce or separation seemed imminent. Rather, the two stopped turning toward each other and began turning away from each other to individual pursuits and interests, family matters at large, or needs that seemed to beckon their attention and care. They neglected the burning coals between them until their passion died out completely.

Josh McDowell once reported the results of a survey of high school students in which 90 percent of the students said they could not imagine their parents having sex.

Does marriage have to degenerate into such a sad state of affairs? No! God has a much different desire for marriage. In His plan, the romance continues throughout the marriage. In fact, it builds and grows into a loving and passionate marriage that is even more wonderful in its latter stages than in its beginning. A marriage that cools and grows stale is not biblical! It is worldly wisdom that makes it acceptable. Rebel against such error!

THE FACTORS THAT KILL ROMANCE

In the book of Revelation, we read about the four horsemen of the apocalypse. I believe there are four horsemen of the apocalypse that relate to marriage:

1. Sin

Romance dies when one or both persons become so wounded and disillusioned with a spouse that they become calloused. Sin and harsh actions are unrepented of until the wounds of sin have removed all feeling. "A brother offended is harder to win than a strong city, and contentions are like the bars of a castle" (Prov. 18:19).

2. Age

Romance dies when a person focuses on the outer beauty rather than on the inner beauty of his or her spouse. Outer beauty degenerates over time; age takes its toll on every person. I don't care how many face or body lifts a person has, or how much a person attempts to keep in shape through proper nutrition and exercise, age causes a fading of physical beauty. Unless you continue to see beyond the wrinkles around your beloved's eyes and gaze into the full depths of your mate's soul, you will feel less attracted to your spouse, and with a lessening of attraction, you are likely to express less romance.

I heard this story of a man who married a beautiful woman. Several years after their wedding, she was in a terrible automobile accident. Her injuries caused a nerve in her face to be damaged so that when she smiled, she appeared disfigured—her mouth drooped significantly to one side. When she realized the permanent nature of her injury, she feared her husband's reaction. She had been raised to place a high value on physical beauty and to work at being beautiful. She couldn't imagine that her husband could continue to love her if she was ugly, which is how she perceived herself in the wake of the accident.

When her husband came into her hospital room after the doctors had removed the bandages from her face, he looked at her and smiled. She smiled back and watched closely for his reaction. He studied her for a moment and then said sweetly and sincerely, "Looks kinda cute." Then he reached down toward her, pursed his lips in a way that nearly mirrored the new shape of her mouth when she smiled, and kissed her gently.

What a loving act on the man's part! What a healing, restorative act for his wife! From that moment, the woman knew with a certainty in her heart that the love of her husband did not depend upon her physical beauty. Any woman who comes to know that truth in her marriage experiences great inner freedom and feelings of value.

3. Forgetfulness

Romance dies when couples forget the preciousness of their mates. Spouses too often come to take each other for granted, and they lose sight of just how special they are to each other. Romance requires intention, care, and focus. It requires that each person keep in active memory what gave birth to the marriage. It requires that each person continue to remember the special traits in the spouse that fueled attraction at the initial stages of their relationship. God calls a man's bride "the wife of your youth" (Mal. 2:14).

4. Laziness

Many people recite vows to "love, honor, and cherish" a spouse, and then they proceed with their marriage without a good knowledge of how to keep them. Love must be shown. Honor must be expressed. Cherish is an attitude that must be displayed. Passionate marriages are so by design and intent. Romance is a discipline.

Couples too often get caught up in routine matters related to family and general living, and they fail to carve out the time and space necessary to do the loving, honoring, and cherishing necessary to keep romance alive. A sexual relationship tends to take care of itself by instinct and intuition. But what happens in all those many hours and minutes that are not associated with sexual intimacy requires effort. The daily chores of life as well as the little expressions of love—such as writing love notes to each other, bringing home flowers, fixing a favorite meal—take thought, time, and effort.

Don't let the four horsemen of the apocalypse descend on your marriage. Choose to remain absolutely faithful to your spouse. Choose to focus on the inner qualities of your spouse and to nurture, edify, and praise them. Choose to recall frequently the things that you admire in your spouse and to recall special moments that have enriched your relationship through the years. Choose to make the effort to show your spouse frequently how much you love, honor, and cherish him or her. "Discipline yourself for the purpose of godliness" (1 Tim. 4:7 NASB).

KEEPING ROMANCE ALIVE IN YOUR MARRIAGE

Solomon and his wife seem to have discovered the secret of a lifelong romance:

> *Come, my beloved,*
> *Let us go forth to the field;*
> *Let us lodge in the villages.*
> *Let us get up early to the vineyards;*
> *Let us see if the vine has budded,*
> *Whether the grape blossoms are open,*
> *And the pomegranates are in bloom.*
> *There I will give you my love.* (Song 7:11–12)

What season were they in? Springtime! They courted and got married in springtime. They were still in springtime years later. They were out on a date!

As we take a closer look at chapter 7 in this amazing book, I want to call your attention to three truths related to romance:

First, men are expected to be romantic. A husband is to lead in this area.

A number of men, old and young, have said to me down through the years, "I'm just not Romeo." Let me assure you of this: whether you consider yourself to be Romeo or not, you have married Juliet. She believes you are capable of being Romeo, or she wouldn't have married you. And furthermore, she continues to expect you to display Romeo qualities. I believe every woman on earth wants to be treated with tenderness, romance, consideration, courtesy, etiquette, and delicate care. I don't care if she wrestles at the sports arena on weekends. Once she is at home and with her man, she wants tenderness and romance. She is Juliet in her heart. Do your utmost to be her Romeo.

Second, men are capable of romance. Men tend at times to deny their romantic ability. Let me remind you that the greatest artists, sculptors, chefs, architects, designers, poets, and romantic leads of all time have been men. Most men have at least some ability to express charm, romance, and affection. Go with what you have, and over time, you likely will find more and more ways of expressing romance. An ability to be romantic is like many other abilities—you can learn and grow in your capacity for romance over time.

Third, God desires for men to be romantic. At its core, what is romance? It is expressing tender desire to be with another person and making that person feel special and valuable. Who is our example in expressing romance? God, our loving heavenly Father! He gently woos each of us to receive His love and forgiveness. God infuses within us a sure sense of our identity and value. He is the One who is ever reaching out to us in specific ways to show us how much He loves us, cares for us, and desires to be with us in intimacy of spirit.

Romance ultimately comes down to resolve. I've seen men send flowers to their dates and those they were courting until I thought they would buy out all of Holland, and then once those men were married, their wives never saw another bloom apart from holiday times.

Men tend to throw all of their romantic energy into a few occasions—Christmas, Valentine's Day, the wedding anniversary, the wife's birthday, and sometimes Mother's Day. On these occasions, they back the truck to the door of their marriage and dump a load of chocolates, flowers, or jewelry. All other days of the year, it's business as usual. They are efficient, not creative.

The Spontaneous and Unexpected

Romance is rooted to a marked degree in the spontaneous and unexpected. I frequently advise men to spread out their display of affection over the entire year rather than concentrate so much energy and money on a few events. A marriage relationship needs nourishing, and "frequent feedings" is a good principle to follow. A single flower brought home on a day when you know your wife has struggled, an encouraging and uplifting love note tucked into your husband's briefcase so that he'll find it right before an important meeting, a quick call to say "I love you" on a day when you both have too many things to do—these things seep into the soul of a relationship and create romance.

In a counseling session, a man sincerely asked his wife what she would like for him to do as an indicator that he still loved her. In other words, he was asking, "What would be romantic to you?" She replied, "I'd like for you to pick me up."

He immediately grabbed her to "heft" her up.

"No," she said with a sigh, "*pick* me up, just like you did that day when we met at the country dance hall."

She wanted her husband to flirt with her.

The next Saturday night, he took his wife out dancing to a new country dance place in their town, and he told me later, "We just sat there and made eyes at each other. That tickled her."

Now that was a smart guy. He was a welder by trade, a real man's man, not at all the type of person you would think could be so romantic. Yet deep down inside, he admitted that he enjoyed what happened on Saturday night as much as his wife enjoyed it. Something youthful and passionate had been rekindled in each of them. Their marriage had been fed a healthy dose of romance.

Continue to Date

I encourage all married couples to continue to date throughout their marriage. Set aside specific time to spend together, and then don't let other things become a higher priority. Teresa and I go out on Wednesday nights. I shut down everything else, and unless an emergency arises and I have Teresa's consent to deal with it in place of our date, I spend Wednesday evening exclusively with my wife. We usually go out to the restaurant of her choice, and over dinner together, I make every attempt I can to be a good listener and to devote my full attention to her. In other words, I make sure the TV set is behind *me,* not behind her.

This is not a casual thing with us, in which we say to each other, "Well, let's take a break and go out." It's a planned event.

Men, going on a date means that you shower, dress up a little, brush your teeth, and truly get ready for a special evening. In doing so, you are sending a message to your wife that you consider this to be valuable and special time together.

When you are out with your wife at a restaurant, don't stare out the window while she eats her salad. Gaze into her eyes. Close out all others unless you mutually agree to "people watch" together. Listen to what your wife wants to say to you. Display your very best manners. Be courteous, respectful, and tender with your wife. Few things are as arousing as manners. Make her feel like the most important person in the world to you—and do it with a genuine heart. Set aside the time from 7:30 to midnight for the two of you alone. You'll be glad you did.

"But what about the children?" you may ask. Certainly I believe that you and your spouse should do things as a family. Set aside another night each week that you consider to be an inviolable family night. These evenings and weekend events with your family, however, should be in addition to your date night with your wife.

Some have asked me, "But won't the children feel resentful and left out?" Your children will understand the idea of Mom and Dad being on a date, and in later years, they will highly value the fact that you spent that time alone together and they will want to model such behavior in their lives. I have met countless young people who resent the fact that their parents were away from home on business trips or stayed late at work too often, or that one parent went out by himself to drink, party, or play cards, leaving the other spouse and children at home. I have never met a young person who was resentful that his or her parents went out on a date once a week. Rather, they seem always to recall that as evidence that the foundation of their home life was loving and strong. Later in life, these children brag about their parents' romance.

Setting aside a night a week to be with your spouse sends a strong message to your spouse, to your children, and to anyone else who may be observing your marriage that you value your spouse as a person and you value your relationship. It is a strong sign of "love, honor, and cherish."

A fellow pastor told me a story from the days in which he was involved in the Fellowship of Christian Athletes (FCA). One of the basic elements of an FCA meeting is to have a "huddle group" in which a small group gathers for Bible study and prayer. This man became so involved in FCA that he was going out nearly every night to an FCA meeting. One night as he left the house, his wife looked at him with tears in her eyes and asked, "What about *our* huddle group?"

He said to me, "That froze me in my boots. I got in my car and drove through tears all the way to that high school. The next day I called my supervisor and said, 'I'm giving up some of my commitments.' I started giving my time to ministry at home, and over the years, I've realized that ministry at home is not only as valid, but perhaps even more valid than any form of ministry done outside the home. Having a huddle group with my wife, and later my children, is a key part of our family life."

Husband, you *can* be romantic. God desires for you to be romantic, and it's up to you to take the lead in romance in your marriage. Early on, it was your instinct to be romantic. Later, it must become a discipline.

GREATER APPRECIATION THAN EVER BEFORE

Let's take a close look at what happens in chapter 7 of the Song of Solomon. They were back in the bedroom again! Solomon said, "How beautiful are your feet in sandals, O prince's daughter!" (Song 7:1).

On their wedding night, Solomon began his exclamation

of love by starting at the top of his bride's head. His first comments to her were about her eyes, her hair, her smile, her blushing cheeks. (See Song 4:1–3.) Now, at a more mature stage in their marriage, Solomon began at her feet. To make such a statement to his wife, Solomon very likely was on his knees before her, holding her feet in his hands as he unwrapped the thongs of her sandals. In essence, he was bowing before his wife. We've all heard the statement, "He worships the ground she walks on." Well, this is not a far cry from what Solomon was doing. He was showing a tremendous sign of respect to his wife. He was not demanding that she bow before him; rather, he was on his knees before her.

In Bible times, it was customary for a servant to take off the shoes of the master or mistress of a home and then to bathe the person's feet in a basin of water. Wealthy homes and palaces, such as Solomon's, were carpeted with beautiful handmade carpets, large and small, often layered for added softness. One generally went barefoot in such a home. Solomon was serving his wife just as a servant might have.

Let me point out one other thing related to sandals. Sandals were worn by those who were trusted to leave the confines of a home or palace. Slaves were kept barefoot, and so were the women in the harems of wealthy or powerful men. Solomon trusted his wife explicitly to come and go from his presence. He neither controlled nor confined her. He had total faith that she would behave in an honorable manner when she was away from their home, and that she would return to him. He trusted her to appear publicly without him, knowing he could rely on her to be loyal to him and to bring honor to his name. As Proverbs 31:11 tells us, "The heart of her husband safely trusts her." An overly controlling man is a man who does not trust his wife. Such a lack of trust is demeaning and dishonoring to her.

What tremendous insight we have about this woman! She

was utterly trustworthy and honorable. How beautiful were her feet in sandals! She carried a dignity, grace, and elegance wherever she went, and she reflected well her devotion to Solomon.

There was nobility in what Solomon said by calling his wife a "prince's daughter." In the Proverbs of Solomon we find this statement:

> *Her children rise up and call her blessed;*
> *Her husband also, and he praises her:*
> *"Many daughters have done well,*
> *But you excel them all."* (Prov. 31:28–29)

That was how Solomon felt about his wife. He was proud of her. She was his crown, the display of his worth.

One night not long ago, I was sitting in my recliner, and I called to my wife, Teresa, "Come here, Sweetie." I sat her on my lap and put my arms around her and looked deeply into the eyes of this woman to whom I have been married more than twenty years. I said, "I want you to know, Honey, that you have never embarrassed me. You are a pride to me, a pride to our sons. You are a precious daughter of God." I only got about that far before I started to cry. I've never been embarrassed to cry in front of my wife. My tears are a sign not of weakness to her, but of sincerity and strength of conviction. As far as I am concerned, my wife "excels them all." She is my one and only. And I'm not at all ashamed to let her know that I appreciate her.

Wife, be to your husband the kind of woman that Solomon's wife was to him. Make your husband proud of you in all that you do. Husband, be the kind of man to your wife that Solomon was to his wife—be willing to serve her and to praise her. Do what Proverbs 31:31 teaches: "Give her of the fruit of her hands." Praise is payday.

ACKNOWLEDGE THE BEST IN YOUR SPOUSE

Solomon did not end his expression of appreciation for his wife at her feet. That was only the beginning. He moved up her body and observed,

> *The curves of your thighs are like jewels,*
> *The work of the hands of a skillful workman.*
> *Your navel is a rounded goblet;*
> *It lacks no blended beverage.*
> *Your waist is a heap of wheat*
> *Set about with lilies.* (Song 7:1–2)

I want to point out two key things about these compliments that Solomon gave to his wife:

First, Solomon complimented what he alone knew to be true about his wife. Wives in Solomon's time didn't wear bikinis to the beach. A woman's body belonged exclusively to her husband and was for his pleasure alone. No man other than her husband saw her upper legs and abdomen.

In a good marriage, there are going to be some things that only a wife should know about a husband, and a husband about a wife—some of those things are going to be flaws, some are going to be the hidden strengths and talents that the world has failed to appreciate. Solomon focused totally on the positive. He never mentioned a single flaw in his bride. He praised her good qualities and brought them to her attention. It was as if he were saying to her, "Honey, I know how wonderful you are. It doesn't matter if nobody else in the world understands all of the goodness that is present in you. I know. And I'm here to tell you that you are perfection in my eyes."

Second, Solomon complimented more than just his wife's physical attributes. What did Solomon praise about his wife? Not only did he admire her body and its sensual curves. He also admired her strength. In the Bible, the upper legs are used as a symbol for steadfast loyalty and strength. The woman was strong in character, and she carried her strength in a beautiful way. In other words, she had inner strength clothed in graciousness. She didn't buckle under pressure or fall apart in a crisis. She didn't burst into anger or rage, or go into hysterics, when things didn't go her way. Her bearing communicated, "I know who I am in the Lord, and I am going to endure to the end in my faith and in my loyalty to my husband. I will not be moved from righteousness. I will stand for what is good and noble, and I will speak and act in a way that others appreciate and admire."

Solomon admired her fruitfulness. Both wheat and wine are signs of harvest—wheat is harvested in the spring and wine is the result of a fall harvest of grapes. Solomon was conveying, "From beginning to end, you have been fruitful and diligent in your giving to me and to others." She was indeed the crown of a proud husband.

A PERCEPTION OF CONTINUED YOUTH

In continuing to move up the body of his wife, Solomon said this about her breasts: "Your two breasts are like two fawns, twins of a gazelle" (Song 7:3). That was *exactly* what he said to her about her breasts on their wedding night. In saying that at that point in their marriage, Solomon conveyed two messages:

First, Solomon admired his wife's ongoing youthfulness. In reality, her breasts might not have been sleek and taut as a gazelle in flight, but Solomon saw in his wife a youthfulness of spirit that continued to fill her being. She was forever young in his eyes.

Second, Solomon admired his wife's responsiveness to him. She was still bashful in his sight, and yet quick to respond to his touch. He delighted in the fact that he could still sexually excite her.

No matter how old a woman may get, she can still have a youthful spirit about her, and she can still be responsive to her husband—traits that delight a man and give him a renewed sense of his youth and ability to perform sexually. The fire definitely had not gone out between those two. In the way they loved each other, they might as well have been newlyweds. They desired each other, and each had a keen awareness of what would delight the other.

Certain things about sexual intimacy may change over time. Some aspects of lovemaking may take a little longer, for example, but every couple can maintain a desire for each other and a delight in each other. If, as a couple, each has a desire for and a delight in the other, you will experience a "forever young" aspect to your sexual union, regardless of how old you are in physical years.

A woman once said to me, "I'm a nurse and I work in a nursing home. Two of the people who live in this particular home have been married to each other for seventy years. They are both in their nineties now, and they get around in wheelchairs. The casual visitor might think they are weak and frail and beyond any feelings of sexual desire. But you should see how they look at each other! They may not share a common bed, but they still hold hands and kiss and flirt with each other in a way that can almost make a person feel embarrassed to watch them. There is no doubt they are still very much in love and that the feelings they have for each other are sexual as well as emotional. They still have the hots for each other."

May it be so for every married couple!

APPRECIATION FOR THE TOTAL PERSON

I want you to notice specifically what Solomon said about his wife's neck and head. He pointed out four features:

Your neck is like an ivory tower,
Your eyes like the pools in Heshbon
By the gate of Bath Rabbim.
Your nose is like the tower of Lebanon
Which looks toward Damascus.
Your head crowns you like Mount Carmel,
And the hair of your head is like purple;
A king is held captive by your tresses. (Song 7:4–5)

A Tower of Strength and Purity

First, Solomon referred to his wife's neck as a tower. On their wedding night, as he was taking off her wedding necklace, he saw her neck as a tower of strength for fending off all enemies. Now, Solomon saw his wife's neck as a white tower—great in strength and in value, but also a symbol of purity. She had borne her strength of character as well as her inner pride at being Solomon's wife with a purity of heart. She had not trampled over others or sought vengeance against others. Rather, she stood tall and proud in her position as Solomon's wife. She always had a regal dignity about her.

A Depth of Holiness and a Source of Refreshment

Second, Solomon referred to his wife's eyes as deep pools of water. You can tell a great deal about a person by gazing deeply into the eyes. What did Solomon see in his wife's eyes? He spoke of the Bath Rabbim pools near Heshbon. The city of Heshbon was a Levitical city—in other words, it was a city in which the priests dwelled. Solomon saw holiness in the eyes of his wife. Furthermore, the pools were very likely the pools in which the priests purified themselves ceremonially before and after their service as priests. Solomon saw his wife as being completely cleansed of all sin. She stood in righteousness and purity before the Lord. Nothing in her was tainted by guile, sin, or guilt.

In addition to being a means of cleansing, pools of water are sources of refreshment, and perhaps especially so since the city and the pools were out in the desert area, about twenty miles east of the north end of the Dead Sea. Solomon seemed to take delight in the "refuge" of his wife—the refreshment she gave to his soul and the delight she provided him at the end of a hard day of work.

Show me a man who can go home from work to a wife who is pure and holy before God, and who gives him refreshment and joy, and I'll show you a man who is eager to get home!

A Strong Ally Against Trouble

Third, Solomon referred to her nose as a tower of Lebanon looking toward Damascus. Damascus was the seat of power for Assyria, a major enemy to the Israelites throughout Bible times. Solomon regarded his wife as always being on the alert to the things that might bring trouble to him. In our terms today we might say, "She looks out for her husband." She wasn't about to let another woman get his attention or draw him away. She wasn't about to let someone willingly hurt her husband or damage his reputation. The wife no doubt was also looking out for her husband through intercessory prayer on his behalf. She was aware that he had enemies—both in the natural and in the spiritual realms—and she set herself to be his foremost lookout post.

Someone once said to me, "This woman had a nose for sniffing out trouble." Precisely. She wasn't eager for trouble, but she was always alert to potential trouble. Her husband saw her as a strong pillar of first-line defense! In all of my years of ministry, I have found no greater counsel and wisdom than that of my sweetheart.

A Visibly Good Leadership

Fourth, Solomon noted that his wife's hair was like a crown. As a young bride, she let her tresses fall down around her shoulders. Solomon observed that her hair was cascading like a flock of goats running down a mountain. Perhaps now she had her hair up and perhaps braided in such a way that it was like a crown on her head. Purple, of course, was the color for royalty in the Bible, and that was what Solomon saw in his wife's appearance at that stage of her life. She was truly a queen, worthy at all times of wearing a royal crown.

Solomon likened her carriage to the hills of Carmel, the showplace for geographic beauty in Israel. It was a prized fertile area that everyone agreed was the most beautiful part of the land. On Mount Carmel the prophet Elijah showed forth the power of God against the priests of Baal. It was a place visible for miles and miles from the valleys that extended below it to the east. Solomon saw his wife as being worthy of much public acclaim. Queens wore their crowns only at royal, public events. Solomon saw his wife as being worthy of recognition as a righteous queen at all times.

Husband, always treat your wife as the queen of your home. Be as totally captivated by her as Solomon was captivated by his wife. Solomon was the most powerful man in the world of his time. And yet, his wife owned him. She truly was the strength behind the throne, the strong woman behind the strong man. The New Testament term for "housewife" is *oikodespotes*—"house despot"! She was monarch of the realm. (See 1 Tim. 5:14.)

At a conference I attended, the speaker's words made a strong impression on me: "All of my married life, my wife loved me and cared for me and looked after me. She was my crown and my praise. People held me in much higher regard than they otherwise would have because of her reputation for excellence and the way she built me up in their eyes. Now my wife is dying. Her mind has been affected, and at times, I'm not even sure she knows who I am. But now it's my turn to serve. I bathe her, I change the diapers she must wear, and I hold her withered body in my arms and cuddle her and tell her that I love her. I consider it the greatest privilege God has ever given me to do for this woman just a fraction of what she has done for me in my life, and to love her with a devotion that is only a small reflection of the devoted love she expressed for me."

Solomon seemed to feel the same way about his wife: "How fair and how pleasant you are, O love, with your delights!" (Song 7:6). One of the meanings of the word *delight* is "charm." Solomon was totally under the spell of his wife; he was fully captivated by her. Though king of his domain, he is enslaved by the delight of his wife. He tried to summarize the totality of her being to him: "This stature of yours is like a palm tree, and your breasts like its clusters" (Song 7:7).

Solomon initially called his young bride a garden. Now he had come to see her as an oasis in the desert. She was a place of rest, refreshment, and nourishment to him—still a delight, but in a different way. At the beginning of their marriage, Solomon was attracted to the beauty and intrigue and bloom of his young bride as well as to her potential. At the later stage of their marriage, Solomon was no less attracted, but he was attracted to different things: his wife's stateliness and fruitfulness to his life. The younger groom Solomon was eager for what his wife would give him. The older husband Solomon was grateful and appreciative for all that his wife gave him. Of all the people on earth, he most longed to come to her. A man told me, "My home is wherever my wife happens to be at the time." That was how Solomon felt. His wife was his place of refuge and pleasure.

APPRECIATION EXPRESSED IN TENDER WORDS

Up to this point in the seventh chapter of the Song of Solomon, Solomon was talking, not touching. He was praising his wife for what he saw in her, not for what he could get from her. Oh, that all men might master this fine art! This is truly one of the greatest secrets of romance.

Romance is about *giving* to another person. It is about appreciating that person and valuing that person. It is about showing signs of respect and trust. It is about admiration.

Romance is also about tenderness. Solomon began with tender and romantic words in communicating his love to his wife, and men, that is always the place to begin with your wives. They want to know how you feel in your heart, not how you respond to the feel of them in your hand.

Remain Tender

The way a woman spells love over time is *tenderness.* The way a man spells love over time is *respect.*

Show me a woman who feels that her husband deals with her tenderly—with kindness, good manners, generosity, genuine affection, and understanding—and I'll show you a happily married woman, regardless of external circumstances that may come against their union or family. This woman will have no desire to seek tenderness from someone outside the marriage.

Show me a husband who feels that his wife deals with him with respect—admiration, appreciation, upholding his dignity as a man, thankful for his protection and provision—and I'll show you a happily married man, regardless of the stress he may feel from the outside world. This man will delight in coming home and closing the front door behind him so that he can be with his wife and family.

What happens if tenderness isn't there for a woman? She'll begin to withdraw from her husband. Eventually she may cut off all sexual responsiveness to him. She may withdraw silently, but very often, her withdrawal is punctuated with criticism, manipulation, and angry remarks. She will eventually turn to other avenues for feeling rewarded, appreciated, or important. It may be a job; it may be a full schedule of civic volunteer work; it may be spending more time with her mother or her friends; it may be excessive devotion to the kids or even a passion for church work. She'll find a tenderness substitute for what is lacking at home.

And then one day she may be by herself at a cafe somewhere, and a guy at the next booth will say, "Hi, ya." She will say, "Hi, ya," back. "Come here often?" he'll ask. "Oh, usually on Tuesdays," she'll say. She might never have been there on a Tuesday before, but she has made a mental plan to be there *next* Tuesday. And he knows it. "Maybe I'll see ya," he'll say, fully intending to be at the cafe next Tuesday. And so it goes. What is she after? A tenderness fix. Somebody to listen, to understand, to admire her, to show that he likes being with her and finds her appealing.

The beginning of a very rough time has started in such a marriage—not with the fantasy or encounter she has with another person—but with the lack of tenderness shown to her initially by her husband.

Remain Respectful

And from the man's point of view? If he doesn't receive respect at home, he'll seek it out. Often, he'll seek it out at work, spending longer and longer hours on the job where he seems to be appreciated and valued and the rewards seem possible to achieve. He may spend more time with his friends and start driving a fancier car and unbuttoning his shirt to his navel so people might be impressed with his illusion of youth. One day he'll come across a woman who will be quick to adore him, saying, "You are so sharp!" He'll take the bait. "You really think so?" he'll reply modestly, all the while begging in his heart for more.

The more this husband withdraws from his family and seeks respect outside the home, the more disrespect he is likely to feel from his wife, and so the cycle escalates.

The beginning of a very difficult time in that marriage has started—not with the infidelity and abandonment, but with the lack of respect shown by the wife.

I was giving this teaching at a church one time, and after the service a man in his forties came up to me and said, "Did my mother write you a letter?" He felt as if I had just told his life story. No, I had never met him before, and I had received no correspondence from his mother. The pattern is a frequent one. I have seen it all too often, in various stages of development, in my pastoral counseling over the past twenty years.

When husbands fail in tenderness and wives fail to show respect, marriages wither. Revere your mate. If you don't, Satan will find someone who will.

APPRECIATION EXPRESSED IN TENDER EMBRACE

Solomon, however, was not all talk. He also expressed his love for his wife in deed:

> *I said, "I will go up to the palm tree,*
> *I will take hold of its branches."*
> *Let now your breasts be like clusters of the vine,*
> *The fragrance of your breath like apples,*
> *And the roof of your mouth like the best wine.* (Song 7:8–9)

The woman responded:

> *The wine goes down smoothly for my beloved,*
> *Moving gently the lips of sleepers.* (Song 7:9)

This is a picture of two people overcome by wine. Not the wine of drunkenness but the wine of passion and love. They sleep the restful sleep of a contented couple. Palm clusters, apples, wine—Solomon's wife was an absolute delight to him, an oasis of refreshment. He adored her breasts, breath, mouth, and lips. A strong sexual expression is evident here. To pollinate a palm tree, one would climb the tree and seize the flowers. So Solomon here entered his wife. Is this the dying of romantic love? Not on your life!

YOU BECOME WHAT YOU GIVE

Solomon told his wife all that was in his heart about her. An important message was in the overall statement that he made to his wife. Solomon ascribed to his wife the very traits he himself most respected and desired to have in his life. He wanted to be, as a man, the type of person he saw in his wife: strong, noble, fruitful, youthful, generous, alert, righteous, regal.

A truly good marriage has that uplifting and encouraging aspect to it—each person bringing out and strengthening the best in the other, each person being the type of person he or she would also like to be. I heard an interview with a couple not long ago, and the wife concluded, "It may sound corny, but he really does bring out the highest in me. I'm hoping that I become more and more like him." That's what a good marital relationship should be like. I know that my wife is one of my heroes.

Solomon knew that his wife enriched his life by her

presence and that she blessed his life with her goodness so that he was a better man than he was when he first married her. That was part of the reason he used the image of an oasis. As he held her, he knew that she was a great source of "soul food" for him—grapes, apples, and wine were all indicative of the way he felt nourished by his wife so that he became what she fed to him emotionally.

A spouse always has it in his or her power to determine what kind of emotional nourishment will be given in a marriage. Will you feed your mate a diet of angry words, bitter insults, or negative put-downs? Or will you feed your mate a diet of genuine compliments, encouragement, and statements of value? What you feed your spouse is likely to be what you are fed in return. And in this case, you truly do become what you eat. A person who receives mostly anger, bitterness, and hate at home is going to express anger, bitterness, and hate to the world. A person who receives unconditional love, appreciation, respect, and tenderness at home is going to give the same things to others.

Solomon knew that. He was a better king for having had the woman as his queen.

A ROMANTIC RESPONSE

You may be thinking, *But how did she feel about Solomon?* Was the romance flowing only one way? Far from it!

Solomon's bride responded, "I am my beloved's, and his desire is toward me" (Song 7:10). The word *desire* is used in Genesis 4:7 of an animal prepared to devour its prey. As in the previous verses, Solomon wanted to consume the woman of delight. Passion indeed!

His wife, after all those years of marriage, still considered herself to be a one-man woman, and she delighted in the fact that he was a one-woman man when it came to the fullness of his love and devotion. She considered herself to be one with him. She delighted in his incredible passion. She purposefully excited him and was proud of it.

I asked my wife, Teresa, one time what happens when women get older. I said, "Men get rigid and robotic. We start operating by rote. What is it that women become?"

She replied, "We get fussy. We have no tolerance for things not being done our way."

We reflected upon those statements for a while and came to two conclusions: (1) these traits do not necessarily need to develop, and (2) these traits develop because people become self-centered and self-focused. They increasingly want what they want, to the exclusion of others.

Solomon's wife displayed none of this attitude. She remained focused on Solomon. And that perhaps is the greatest fruit of romance. When a person chooses to love and appreciate another through gestures, deeds, and words that we would call romantic, the response is a spouse who is more giving and loving in return. There is a reciprocity of affection and a mutuality of caring.

Notice what the wife said next:

> *Come, my beloved,*
> *Let us go forth to the field;*
> *Let us lodge in the villages.*
> *Let us get up early to the vineyards;*
> *Let us see if the vine has budded,*
> *Whether the grape blossoms are open,*
> *And the pomegranates are in bloom.* (Song 7:11–12)

She was saying, "Let's spend time together. Let's be involved in work and ministry together. Wherever you're going, I want to go along. I want to be with you."

Their love was very much *alive.* She still wanted to be with her husband more than she wanted to be with anybody else. She delighted in his presence. Having him around was not a burden to her, but a joy. She was willing to go where he wanted to go and to work by his side.

Notice, too, that they are springtime images:

> *There I will give you my love.*
> *The mandrakes give off a fragrance,*
> *And at our gates are pleasant fruits,*
> *All manner, new and old,*
> *Which I have laid up for you, my beloved.* (Song 7:12–13)

Mandrakes and "pleasant fruits" refer to aphrodisiacs. (See Gen. 30:14.) Solomon's wife responded to his romantic gestures and deeds with a strong desire to make love to her husband. She had some pleasures for him both "new and old." She was still willing to experiment in the bedroom. She had some surprises remaining in her storehouse of creativity for Solomon.

A number of years ago, my wife, Teresa, and I went on a Caribbean cruise. Our luggage seemed to be misplaced at the outset of the voyage, and we faced the hard, cold fact that we might be several days on the ship with only the clothes we had on our backs. I tried to comfort Teresa by saying, "I've got enough money with me that we can buy the things we need once we stop at the first island." She could not be consoled. Finally, in tears, she said, "But I had a special red nightgown just for tonight."

I went straight to the captain of that ship and said, "I want my luggage! Find it *now*!" I was not about to be denied that red nightgown and my wife in it! She had "something new" for me, and I was ready to receive it. (They did find our luggage, by the way. I sang a new song. . . .)

Wife, never lose sight of the fact that you can still be even more creative in your lovemaking. Your husband will delight in the fantasies you create and the innovations you bring to sexual intimacy. Lay up some "new treasures" for your husband to enjoy. Exploit your husband. All senses delight him. In order of what excites men most:

1. What he hears during sex.
2. What he sees. Trust me, he longs to give you a gift certificate to Victoria's Secret.
3. What he feels, *especially* the responsiveness of his wife.
4. What he smells.
5. What he tastes.

Wife, use the whole arsenal at your disposal!

WHO CARES WHO KNOWS!

Solomon's wife seemed to make a strange statement at the height of her response to Solomon's romantic lead:

Oh, that you were like my brother,
Who nursed at my mother's breasts!
If I should find you outside,
I would kiss you;
I would not be despised.
I would lead you and bring you
Into the house of my mother,
She who used to instruct me.
I would cause you to drink of spiced wine,
Of the juice of my pomegranate.

His left hand is under my head,
And his right hand embraces me. (Song 8:1–3)

On the surface, it may sound as if she was saying at the outset of chapter 8, "Let's just be friends. Let's be like brother and sister." I overheard a young man make this wry comment, "The three worst words a guy can hear from a girl he is dating are, 'Let's be friends.'" Let me assure you quickly, Solomon's wife didn't want to cool off their passion to a platonic state. Far from it!

She was saying, "I wish I could love you in public with the same passion I have for you in private. I'd like to love you passionately twenty-four hours a day and in every setting of life."

In Bible times, the only men that a woman could touch in public were her father and her brothers. She wasn't allowed to be seen touching her husband because touching between spouses was perceived to be sexual in nature, and therefore, such touching was not something the public should see. She said, "If you were my brother, nobody would think twice about my kissing you in public. Nobody would think twice about our going into a house alone together. I wish I could show you how much I love you without any regard to others."

I certainly am not advocating outrageous public displays of affection between married couples. There are a time and a place for everything. My wife cannot stand to see couples paw at each other in public, and I've come to appreciate her point of view. At the same time, there should be enough passion in a marriage that both spouses would like for there to be no off-limits to their lovemaking. She had an around-the-clock romantic inclination toward her husband, so much so that she said that she would love to *cause* him to "drink of spiced wine, of the juice of my pomegranate." She desired that Solomon be constantly intoxicated by the thought of her sexuality. She would like to be able to seduce him at any place, at any time.

Now, this does not mean that a couple should be experiencing a peak sexual interest twenty-four hours a day, every day of the year for the rest of their marriage. It does mean that there should be times when this kind of passion is expressed. Solomon didn't spend every hour of every day adoring his wife's body or making love to her. She didn't delight in lovemaking every second of every minute. The foundation for their marriage was so strongly rooted in all the right things, however—love, tenderness, respect, affection, courtesy, appreciation—that passion readily bubbled up.

THE ELEMENT OF GOOD SURPRISE

Shakespeare wrote:

So am I as the rich, whose blessed key
Can bring him to his sweet up-locked treasure,
The which he will not every hour survey,
For blunting the fine point of seldom pleasure.
Therefore are feasts so solemn and so rare,
Since, seldom coming, in the long year set,
Like stones of worth they thinly placed are,
Or captain jewels in the carcanet.
So is the time that keeps you as my chest,
Or as the wardrobe which the robe doth hide,
To make some special instant special blest,
By new unfolding his imprison'd pride,
Blessed are you, whose worthiness gives scope,
Being had, to triumph, being lack'd, to hope.

What was Shakespeare saying? He was likening passion to a treasure chest filled with jewels. You don't wear all your jewels or even stare at them all the time. Otherwise, you lose appreciation for them. They are worn at feasts only, and in that regard, they are special in part because they are associated with special occasions.

This same thing holds true in romance. An appealing aspect of romance is that it is *unexpected.*

I once wrote a love note to my wife, Teresa, in which I told her at fairly great length how much I appreciate her, value her, and consider her to be a treasure to me, our sons, and our church. I wrote the note late one Saturday night, and then I tucked it into her Bible at the location of the text for my sermon the following morning. I knew she'd find it when she opened her Bible. And sure enough, it was all I could do to keep preaching as I watched her open the note and read through it. The look she gave me from her pew was one of the most wonderful looks a guy can ever see. Believe me, she energized my sermon! Part of the romance of that love note was that it was unexpected.

A man or woman will quickly realize in marriage that much of every day is devoted to chores. There is not much romance associated with the work of taking care of a home, children, cars, or yards—unless, that is, you choose to add an unexpected element to a specific chore. A man once said to me, "One of the most romantic things I ever did for my wife was to clean up the dishes after a dinner party while she went to take a hot, soaking bath." Doing the unexpected chore as a help to a weary or overstressed spouse can be a very romantic act. A noted female columnist said that to her, "The sound of a vacuum cleaner is foreplay."

If a red nightgown is worn every night, if breakfast in bed is served on a silver tray every morning, if a love note appears in every lunch pail, if a sexy phone call is made every day, the acts cease to become romantic; rather, they are mundane.

Don't allow any single romantic act to be reduced to routine. When was the last time you initiated sex outside the bedroom? "Oh, Tom," you may say, "we're *adults.*" May I remind you that Solomon's wife was also an adult! Stay creative. At the heart of romance is God's creative spirit. God's principles are always true and absolute; nothing about His character changes. God's methods are always new; they are different in every situation. (See Lam. 3:22–23.)

Stay steadfast in your love for your spouse. But stay innovative in the way you express your love.

Questions to Think About or Discuss

1. *Are there romantic things that the two of you once did but no longer do? Why not?*

2. *Describe an ideal date with your loved one. Why not plan such a date?*

3. *What have you come to appreciate about your beloved that you didn't even know to appreciate at the outset of your relationship? What good things have you learned about your beloved's character over time? How might you express your appreciation in a creative way?*

4. *What would you say in a definitive love note to your beloved? Why not write such a note today?*

Nine

Faithful Commitment

Song of Solomon 8:5–14

Shortly after the release of the first Rocky movie, actor Sylvester Stallone was asked whether he thought boxing was good for physical conditioning. He said, "Boxing is a wonderful sport for conditioning as long as you can holler, 'Cut.'"

That's the way some people seem to approach marriage. They think it's a wonderful state of being as long as you can quickly call it quits if any pain arises.

From 1900 to the present time, the divorce rate in the United States has risen more than 700 percent. In our world today, four out of every ten children born since the 1970s have grown up partially or fully in a single-family home.

I once said to my older son, Benjamin, "When I was growing up, we guys would ask other guys, 'What does your father do?' What do you kids ask each other today?"

He replied, "We ask, 'Are your parents still together?'"

We've come a long way when we no longer wonder what a dad does, but where a dad lives.

When I first began conducting weddings more than twenty years ago, I had no problem at the wedding rehearsals in knowing where the groom's parents and bride's parents were to sit. Today, it's a rare wedding if I have two sets of parents who have not been through a divorce. Trying to figure out where the former spouses and sometimes several stepfathers and step-mothers are to sit can be a real juggling act.

That's not what God intended for marriage. His plan was one spouse for all of life. I sometimes say to future grooms in a premarital counseling session, "When you get married, you get measured for your tux and your coffin at the same time." In other words, you are marrying for life, until you are parted by death.

One of my favorite verses in the Bible to use in premarital counseling is not one you would probably call to mind quickly: "You shall not take the name of the LORD your God in vain" (Ex. 20:7). The reason for this verse? This verse relates not to cursing, as many people seem to think, but to the seriousness of vows that we make in the name of the Lord. When a person in Moses' day took an oath by the name of the Lord, he was evoking God's presence as a party and witness to the vow. It was very serious business to invite God to witness a vow and be party to a covenant and then change one's mind. To do so was to publicly lessen the holiness of the vow.

Any person who enters marriage without a full intent to be faithful to his or her spouse for the rest of his or her life, and to remain married regardless of circumstances—"for better or worse, richer or poorer, in sickness and in health"—should not marry. Marriage is not a temporary driving permit for a spin down life's highway. It is a permanent state of being.

GOD'S OPINION ON DIVORCE

If you want to know God's opinion about divorce, turn to Malachi 2:13–16:

You cover the altar of the LORD with tears,
With weeping and crying;
So He does not regard the offering anymore,
Nor receive it with goodwill from your hands.
Yet you say, "For what reason?"
Because the LORD has been witness
Between you and the wife of your youth,
With whom you have dealt treacherously;
Yet she is your companion
And your wife by covenant.
But did He not make them one,
Having a remnant of the Spirit?
And why one?
He seeks godly offspring.
Therefore take heed to your spirit,
And let none deal treacherously with the wife of his youth.
"For the LORD God of Israel says
That He hates divorce,
For it covers one's garment with violence,"
Says the LORD of hosts.
"Therefore take heed to your spirit,
That you do not deal treacherously."

The people in Malachi's time were upset that the Lord didn't seem to be responding to their tears or their offerings—their acts of religious service—and the reason cited was that they had not been faithful to their wives. Notice that the Lord is always a witness to how you treat your spouse. He was present at your wedding ceremony, and He continues to be an ongoing witness to your vows every day of your married life. God does not desire that you profess fidelity and faithfulness to Him and then deal "treacherously"—in an unfaithful and disloyal manner—

with your spouse. That's blatant hypocrisy in God's eyes. God desires a *faithful commitment* through all the years of a marriage.

A ONENESS OF IDENTITY

The Song of Solomon ends as you would imagine—with faithfulness to the end of life. In the Song of Solomon are several aspects of faithful commitment. The first is a oneness of identity. The question is asked, "Who is this coming up from the wilderness, leaning upon her beloved?" (Song 8:5).

Solomon's wife was unrecognizable as being distinguished from Solomon. They were one in the flesh and one in their place in society. Nobody perceived them as being apart from each other. That does not mean that Solomon's wife lost all of her identity as a person; it meant that nobody would dream of inviting Solomon to a social engagement without also inviting Solomon's beloved wife, and nobody would think of flirting with Solomon because Solomon was committed to his wife and she to him.

We have all known couples who seem to go their separate ways even though they are still technically married. He does his thing, she does her thing, and the two of them rarely do the same thing.

That is not faithful commitment. Marriage calls a person to a oneness of identity with another person.

Paul urged, "Husbands love your wives, just as Christ also loved the church. . . . Husbands ought to love their own wives as their own bodies" (Eph. 5:25, 28). This type of love is very personal. It requires a certain loss of self to take another person so completely into your life that you make the other's concerns equal to your own. That is faithful commitment.

MADE JUST FOR EACH OTHER

Solomon said to his wife, "I awakened you under the apple tree. There your mother brought you forth; there she who bore you brought you forth" (Song 8:5).

Several images are very strong in this verse. The fig tree is a symbol of the entire nation of Israel in the Scriptures; it is also a place of meditation. The apple tree, in contrast, is the tree of love. The imagery of this verse sent the message, "Your mother conceived and birthed you in love *just for me.*" There was a sense of destiny about the love and relationship that Solomon's bride had with Solomon. She saw their relationship as not only God-blessed, but also God-ordained or God-authored. She held the opinion, "Nobody could ever have been more right for me. God selected you to be my husband from your birth."

In a faithful, committed marriage, this idea should take root and grow. If you do not believe that God has brought you together as a couple, and that God engineered all of the circumstances and situations that caused you to meet, fall in love, and grow in your love, then you should not marry. If you cannot look back at your life, and the life of your beloved, and see how God has uniquely prepared you for each other, you should not marry.

Those who are faithfully committed to each other in marriage have a sense that God is in control of every aspect of their lives, and that God has as much concern about who they marry and when they marry as they do.

When I look back over my life, I have a strong feeling that God planned from the time Teresa and I were born that we should be together. There is something divine, holy, supernatural about the joining of our lives. I have the feeling that Adam must have had, knowing that God had prepared

Eve especially for him and then brought Eve to him. Indeed, "what *God hath joined,* let no man put asunder."

A man commented to me, "God gave me the wife I *needed* to have. It hasn't always been easy, but God knew I *needed* just this kind of woman to bring about some changes and growth in me." If you ever question whether you married the right person, adopt that man's attitude. God knows you better than you know yourself, and your spouse may be God's chosen tool for bringing out the very best that He put into you.

SEALED TOGETHER PERMANENTLY

Having a faithful commitment to marriage is like having a permanent seal affixed to each person's life. Solomon's bride declared, "Set me as a seal upon your heart, as a seal upon your arm" (Song 8:6). Seals in Bible times were marks of ownership, of possession, of affiliation. Tamar asked Judah for his seal so that there would be no dispute that he was the father of her child. (See Gen. 38.)

Solomon's bride desired that he be sealed to her in his heart—that he feel inseparably linked to her in his attitude and devotion. She also desired that he be sealed to her on his arm—that there was to be no doubt in the public's mind that Solomon was her man. The seal was twofold: inner feelings and outer behavior. She didn't want any other woman to catch her husband's attention, and she didn't want her husband to be looking at any other woman.

Once you are married, your flirting days are over, except when you flirt with your spouse. There is no taking off your wedding ring so you can pretend to be single for a day, a weekend, or a two-day business trip. I sometimes take off my wedding ring when I work out at the gym because I don't want to scratch it on the weight machines. I have been well trained by my wife to put that ring back on my finger the minute my workout is over! She doesn't want any woman to be confused in her thinking that I might be available or looking for a relationship, and neither do I.

Let me say a word to you men about pornography. There is no place for it in the life of a Christian. Looking at a woman's body on the pages of a magazine for the purpose of your sexual titillation is lust, and lusting after any woman other than your wife is adultery or fornication. Leviticus 18 speaks of adultery as looking on the nakedness of another man's wife. A woman's body is meant only for her husband's eyes. No man is ever to see the naked body of a woman other than his wife.

Don't start the practice of using pornography. It produces nothing good in a marriage. Few things can be more destructive to a wife than to realize that her husband has images of a fantasy woman in his mind and that she is subject to a highly unfair comparison. Nothing is more demeaning to a woman.

Many men think of pornography as an innocent pastime. They can't understand why their wives become upset by this practice. But when I ask them to turn the tables around and imagine how they would feel if their wives spent hours staring at nude pictures of men and wondering what it would be like to have sex with them, they suddenly don't like that idea at all!

Set the seal of your spouse on both your heart and your arm, and don't allow anything or anyone to pry off those seals.

A GOOD TYPE OF JEALOUSY

We often think of jealousy as a negative emotion, but that is probably because many people confuse envy and jealousy. Envy is wanting something that belongs to another person—

you covet a possession or are envious that he won a particular award, owns a certain item, or is married to a certain type of person. Jealousy is wanting what is rightfully yours. Jealousy includes a strong desire to keep others from taking away what you have been given by God.

God is jealous for us. We rightfully belong to Him, not to Satan. He responds with strength against anything and anyone who would try to woo us away from Him or entice us to align ourselves with evil. In that vein Solomon's wife stated,

> *Love is as strong as death,*
> *Jealousy as cruel as the grave;*
> *Its flames are flames of fire,*
> *A most vehement flame.* (Song 8:6)

That is, just as death does not give up its people, so true love does not quit.

Godly jealousy does not result in smothering another person or manipulating him, limiting his freedom, or imposing false guilt upon him. Godly jealousy means that you do your utmost to keep your spouse's attention focused on you. In as many ways as possible, you protect your spouse from any temptation to be unfaithful.

Glen Campbell once released a song with the message, "These are the dreams of the everyday housewife who gave up the good life for me." Jealousy for your spouse does not mean that you insist that your mate give up all interests in order to do solely what you like to do. It does mean that you find areas of mutuality so that most of your activities are things you can do together and enjoy together. My wife has lots of interests, and through the years I've purchased camera equipment, easels and paints, and a wide variety of tools for her. I don't share her passion for taking photos, painting, or building things. But I have gone on trips with Teresa and stood by her side when she took photos. We have gone away on retreats together, during which I read quietly or watched old movies while she painted. As much as possible, I find a way to share the time she spends in her special interests, without feeling any need to engage in those activities.

One person I know has a wife who loves to give dinner parties for her women friends. The parties include playing the game of bridge. This man doesn't enjoy playing cards, and he doesn't particularly like to cook. To share this interest with his wife, he plays host for the dinner party, greeting the guests, making sure they have all they need in the way of food and beverage, and working with his wife to clean up the kitchen and house after the party is over. He enjoys the social aspect of these evenings, plus all the compliments he gets about being such a helpful husband! There is a certain degree of jealousy at work. He has no intent of losing his wife to a phantom lover called bridge parties.

Jealousy doesn't mean that you never give a friendly shoulder hug to another person or that you can't talk to a person of the opposite sex at a public gathering. It does mean that you avoid being alone with a person of the opposite sex and that disclosure of your feelings, dreams, and desires is reserved for your spouse alone. Don't confide in others of the opposite sex (unless you are in a professional counseling session and your counselor happens to be of the opposite sex). Don't eat alone with a person of the opposite sex. Eating together is one of the most intimate things two people can do. You are inviting disaster if you make this a practice.

In converse, make sure that you have a willingness to listen to your spouse's confidences, secrets, dreams, desires, plans, and goals, and that you keep this deeper level of sharing with your spouse confidential within your marriage. Make sure you are available to your spouse for the times when your mate wants to be alone with you or to have dinner with just you.

Be possessive about your marriage relationship. Marriage was meant to be shared by two people, and no more than two people.

AN UNQUENCHABLE PERSEVERANCE

Solomon's wife pointed to yet another aspect of faithful commitment: "Many waters cannot quench love, nor can the floods drown it" (Song 8:7). No matter what happens, no matter how high the tide of calamity rises, no matter what circumstance or situation hits your marriage, choose to persevere through it. Love is meant to be an eternal flame.

Marriage is intended to be an anchor that holds. Just as nothing separates us from the love of Christ, so nothing should separate us from the commitment we make to a spouse. (See Rom. 8:35–38.)

I know a young couple who encountered all kinds of tragedy shortly after they married. They experienced deaths in their extended family, the company for whom the husband worked had serious financial difficulties, and so forth. The good news was that they clung to each other in the midst of the difficult times rather than withdrew into themselves or turned outside their marriage to others. They cared for each other. And their marriage emerged from the season of trouble stronger and more mature than that of many couples who have been married for many years.

Choose to turn toward each other when tragedy or trouble strikes at your family. Choose to comfort each other and to help each other through the crises.

Certainly circumstances can quench a loving relationship. A man who is a philanderer and brings home AIDS can't be trusted in a marriage. A woman who totally abandons her family and disappears into oblivion is not a person with whom a man can live out a marriage relationship. But such cases are extremely rare. In the vast majority of cases—99.99999 percent, I'd estimate—a marriage can survive incredibly bad times if both people are faithfully committed to each other. The problem in our society is that people aren't committed to making a marriage work. They don't expect to do what it takes to make a marriage last. They expect instant and automatic gratification without any effort, any patience, any difficulty. A truly faithful commitment endures and endures and endures all types of trouble, trial, and trauma.

Throughout the Scriptures we are admonished repeatedly to love as God loves. His love is *chesed* in nature—"steadfast lovingkindness." It is love that is loyal and unwavering. It is unconditional and lasting. Ask God to give you a bit of His love for your spouse. Such love is priceless and can never be purchased; it can only be given freely and received gratefully.

A TREASURED POSSESSION

Those who are faithfully committed in marriage regard their marriage as their most priceless possession—a genuine treasure. As Solomon's wife said, "If a man would give for love all the wealth of his house, it would be utterly despised" (Song 8:7). In other words, no amount of money could purchase the love you feel for your spouse or be worth destroying your marriage.

This is an important concept to consider when it comes to the work each partner chooses to do. No job is worth losing your wife, no career is worth losing your husband, regardless of what the world may say to you.

No fling or affair is worth destroying your marriage. No special interest or pursuit is worth damaging your relationship with your spouse.

Those who have lost their marriages nearly always confess to me later, "What I was pursuing wasn't nearly as satisfying as the marriage I gave up."

There are some lessons you don't need or want to learn in your life, and one of them is to know what it means to love and be loved and then to lose that love through negligence, willful disobedience, or wandering lust.

Hold tightly to the precious gift you have been given. Don't allow yourself to become casual or nonchalant about your marriage.

A FOUNDATION FOR FAITHFUL COMMITMENT

When is a single person ready for marriage? This next passage gives the Bible's clearest answer. It relates to the matter of premarital promiscuity. Solomon's wife recalled the protectiveness of her brothers who watched over her:

We have a little sister,
And she has no breasts.
What shall we do for our sister
In the day when she is spoken for?
If she is a wall,
We will build upon her
A battlement of silver;
And if she is a door,
We will enclose her
With boards of cedar.
I am a wall,

And my breasts like towers;
Then I became in his eyes
As one who found peace. (Song 8:8–10)

The idea in this passage is this: if a young woman (or a young man, for that matter) is a wall—shut off to any sexual experience prior to marriage, a closed door to all men, a virgin—then she is worthy to be exalted. She is acknowledged as being capable of becoming the foundation for a strong, beautiful, and valuable marriage. On the other hand, if a woman is a door—swinging herself wide open to any man who might come along—then she should be shut up with boards of cedar. Virginity until marriage is not a divine preference. It is a divine commandment. We fool ourselves when we think otherwise.

The man who marries a virgin goes into marriage with significant trust and faith in his wife. The husband of a virgin can't help reasoning, even subconsciously, "She saved herself for me. If she has that kind of personal discipline and righteousness before marriage, she no doubt will have that kind of personal discipline and righteousness after the wedding is over. She is a woman who will stay faithful to me."

Solomon's wife made a proud claim: "I was a wall. My breasts were towers of defense. I was a virgin. I didn't allow any man to so much as touch me sexually." And what was the result? Solomon saw her as the woman he was to wed. She became to her husband, Solomon, a source of peace. He could trust her completely. He didn't have a moment's worry concerning the possibility she might be unfaithful.

Faithful commitment is much easier if there is strong evidence of both faithfulness and kept commitments in a person's past. If the person you are dating or courting has no strong evidence of faithfulness to others in the past—including honesty, ethical business dealings, and kept promises—reconsider your relationship. Such a person may have trouble keeping the commitments and promises he makes, and enduring in a relationship over time. The last person you want to marry is a fair-weather friend, one who stays around only when things are going his way and all is well. Her brothers' logic was simple: "If you are mature enough to be moral, you are mature enough to be married."

There is a small play on words in this final statement by Solomon's wife, that she "became in his eyes as one who found peace." Solomon's name means "peace"—*shalom,* wholeness, total peace in one's life. She was saying, "He found his inner peace in me; he found his very soul in me."

When will a woman find a husband? God brought Solomon to the woman when she was willing to be single forever rather than sacrifice her purity before God. When she was at that point of willingness, she said, "*Then* I became in his eyes as one who found peace."

What a wonderful feeling, to feel totally at ease and without any doubt about your marriage relationship and the fidelity of your spouse. Truly, it is peace of mind and heart.

The point is that a person is to be what God commands in purity and holiness, and when God is so pleased, then the right person can be brought to him or her.

A friend of mine worked with a young woman in a particular ministry. She often came to him, asking what he thought of a particular guy she was about to date or asking for advice about how she should dress on a date or what she should do in a relationship. One day, this man woke up and asked himself, "What am I looking for in a wife?" He started listing various traits, and the more traits he listed, the more he thought about the young woman. He realized that the girl of his dreams had been right under his nose for months! He proposed to her within a week. For her part, she had loved him in her heart for months and had been waiting patiently for him to wake up and see her with new eyes.

It seemed as if this man made a sudden decision regarding the young woman. In reality, he merely awoke to the fullness of his feelings for her. And that was the message of Solomon's wife—it was as if Solomon suddenly awoke to all that he already felt and was as a man. She completed him and made him realize who he was as a person. He found the very meaning of his name in her.

Become the person God commands you to be, and let Him handle the timing.

MAKING YOURSELF TOTALLY AVAILABLE

Finally, faithful commitment means that you make yourself totally available to your spouse. You don't make plans without taking your spouse into consideration. You don't dream dreams that exclude your spouse. You don't make major decisions without accommodating the needs of your spouse. Solomon's wife announced,

> *Solomon had a vineyard at Baal Hamon;*
> *He leased the vineyard to keepers;*
> *Everyone was to bring for its fruit*
> *A thousand silver coins.*
> *My own vineyard is before me.*
> *You, O Solomon, may have a thousand,*
> *And those who tend its fruit two hundred.*
> *You who dwell in the gardens,*
> *The companions listen for your voice—*
> *Let me hear it!* (Song 8:11–13)

She was describing her life in terms of property. Solomon had vineyards he let out for hire. Her brothers were to watch over Solomon's property and bring its fruits to Solomon. The woman, however, had a sense of ownership over her body. She had her own "vineyard." She said to her husband, "You could have any woman of your choice, but I have only myself to give to you. I have saved myself for you. I can now give myself *completely* to you, with nothing held back from you and no part of me ever given to another." That was total availability!

And who took care of her vineyard, or body? Those brothers whom she thought were angry with her for making her work (Song 1:6) and for setting such firm rules of morality (Song 8:8–9). In the blessedness of marriage, she was deeply appreciative of their efforts. To a young person, a protective parent may seem to hold a harsh stance toward premarital sex, but later in life, if the parent's counsel is followed, that advice will crown the young person with happiness and beauty. Your body will be a worthy vineyard. Incidentally, the vineyard she submitted to work just happened to be Solomon's. Her submission and obedience to what she thought was harsh was a preparation for God's perfect plan.

Furthermore, she longed to hear his voice in her garden. She looked forward to the rewards that would come with loving only one man sexually all her life. She trusted him to be her all in all sexually, and she made herself available to him in the same way. She gave him all that she had, not merely a "tax" or a portion of what she had. She was "old-fashioned." Marriage to her was a total, permanent, giving union.

Not only did she give herself completely in sexual intimacy, but she gave herself completely in all parts of her life. One of the tenderest scenes I have ever witnessed was that of an older woman in my church who sat by her husband's hospital bed and held his hand and stroked it gently until he died. She was there fully, gently and tenderly, until her vow was fulfilled, "until death do us part." She withheld nothing from him, including her time and her devotion.

HURRY HOME, HONEY!

How does this wonderful picture of faithful commitment end? Solomon states, "You who dwell in the gardens, the companions listen for your voice—let me hear it!" He longs to hear his wife call to him to come to her. He longs to love her. He is wanting to drop everything when summoned. Solomon's wife responds,

> *Make haste, my beloved,*
> *And be like a gazelle*
> *Or a young stag*
> *On the mountains of spices.* (Song 8:14)

"Run to me," she said, "swift as a gazelle and strong as a young buck." In other words, "Hurry home to me, Honey! I'm waiting for you, and I'm worth waiting for and running to!" What are the "mountains of spices"? The same, I believe, as twice mentioned previously in this book, the breasts of his wife. Who wouldn't run?

A husband or wife who is faithfully committed to a mate and to the marriage is worthy of running home to embrace. Such a person is a joy to live with and a delight to know in every aspect of "knowing." My wife once read that every husband should have a ten-second kiss upon returning home from work. Praise God for Christian books that give such good advice!

Faithful commitment is not drudgery or an emotional prison cell. It is a release to enjoy the fullness of love and joy in a relationship. With faithful commitment come emotional strength, healing, growth, and peace.

What a wonderful destination point for marriage—to have a hurry-up, I've-got-to-get-home-to-my-beloved attitude toward your spouse, all the days of your life!

May it be so for your marriage—now and always.

Questions to Think About or Discuss

1. *Do both you and your beloved have a long track record in your lives of faithfulness and friendship?*

2. *Do you have a strong sense of destiny that God brought you and your beloved together?*

3. *In what specific ways do you believe you and your beloved complement each other?*

Conclusion

Fresh Beginnings Are Always Possible

All of us are called to manifest divine love to others, especially to our spouses. Our standard is to be the love of God Himself.

Now there are those of you who have read this book and have concluded, "What a standard! I can't possibly reach that standard of love."

You're right. By yourself and in your own power, you cannot. The good news is that you, as a Christian, can live a pleasing life because you are bound to the infinite Spirit of God, who is not bound to human limitations. You can reside in faithfulness, purity, and holiness in all aspects of life because you know that God is dwelling with you and in you and is always there when you call upon Him.

If you do not have a relationship with God, I encourage you to accept the relationship God offers you. God freely offers you His forgiveness and the hope of heaven. All you need to do is to receive His gift—to admit that you are a sinner in need of His forgiveness, to acknowledge the substitutionary death that

Jesus Christ died on the cross, and to receive that provision as being sufficient for your salvation.

I became a Christian during my junior year of college. I was a fallen individual, sinful, lost, condemned, and on my way to eternal punishment. Then a fellow student came into my dorm room and shared with my roommate God's plan for salvation. I listened over his shoulder and realized the simplicity and yet profound wonder of God's provision: Jesus Christ died upon a cross at Calvary for my sin and in my place, and by having faith in His shed blood, I could reach out and receive God's gift of forgiveness and salvation. I knelt and prayed a short time later, "Lord God, I have sinned. I am empty and can't make it on my own. I ask You to forgive me of my sins and to come into my life. I take Jesus as my Savior. I am going to quit trying to live on my own, and I choose instead to put my trust in You." I received Christ. From that moment, old things passed away and all things became new.

The wonderful hope of God's love is that at any time in our lives, if we come to God with a sorrowful, humble heart, He will forgive us and create in us a new opportunity, a clean slate, a new beginning.

God does not love us because we are spotless; rather, He loves us because we are His creations and He forgives us because we have placed our trust in His Son, the spotless Savior. You cannot save yourself. God knows that. He sent His Son to do the job.

HOPE FOR A BETTER FUTURE

A man was baptized in a river, and as the preacher immersed him into the water and lifted him back to his feet, he said, "Your sins are washed away." The man replied, "God help the fish."

You may be feeling that way today. As you have read this book, you may have found yourself saying, "I've really blown it. I've really messed up with God."

The good news is that Jesus Christ died upon a cross for *all* of our sins. No matter how many times you have sinned or how foul in nature your sins may have been, God desires to forgive you and set you on a new path.

Peter came to Jesus one day and asked, "How often should we forgive those who sin against us?" Jesus answered, "Seventy times seven." His answer was a shorthand way of saying, "*Every* time the person sins against you." If God expects and enables us to forgive other people for *all* of their transgressions against us, surely God the Father stands ready to forgive us each and every time we fail, confess our sins to Him, and ask Him to forgive us and help us to live repentant and renewed lives.

Ask God to forgive you. And then receive His forgiveness and move forward in your life, trusting that the slate has been wiped clean and you are free of your past nature and sin.

The Holy Spirit has been given to us as believers in Christ Jesus to help us do the right things and obey God not only in our hearts and attitudes, but also in our words and deeds.

Ask God by His Holy Spirit to help you discern His will and then have the courage to do it. Ask Him to help you change your bad habits and transform your thinking and attitudes into those that conform to His Word.

START OVER

Start over from where you are right now. If you have been sexually promiscuous in the past, choose to be chaste and pure from this point forward.

If you are living with someone outside the vows of marriage, break off the living arrangement. One of you needs to move out. You need to create a new environment for a proper courtship. If you have made a mistake in your past, trust God to forgive you, to cleanse you fully of that mistake, and to prepare you for the spouse He has for you in your future. Rise from your knees forgiven, but sin no more. Pour your ointment on His feet and weep. Rise as the apostle Matthew once rose from his tax office and followed Jesus unreservedly to a new life.

To those who are divorced, I offer the same encouragement. Ask God to forgive you of your past and to help you learn from your mistake, to cause you to mature in your faith, and to prepare you for the future He has for you.

AIM FOR GOD'S HIGHEST

If you feel as if God has set the standard too high for you to ever reach it, even though you have experienced God's forgiveness for your sinful nature, my advice to you is, "Give it your best effort, and trust God to help you."

If you fail again, ask for God's forgiveness again, give His commandments your best effort, and trust God to help you. Never give up on God's ability to forgive. Never quit when it comes to obedience. Why? Because you must never give up on God's indwelling presence to help you obey and to be transformed in your innermost being so that you will exhibit godly character and right behavior.

Continually seek God's best, and above all, continually seek God. He is your Helper in any time of trouble, in any decision, and in any relationship.

God desires for you to experience the fullness of joy made possible through love, sexual intimacy, and romance. Trust God to help you find and develop a relationship that is anchored in Him. And then enjoy to the maximum His wonderful gift to you!

To Order Video and Audio Material

The Book of Romance is based on a teaching series by Tommy Nelson entitled "The Song of Solomon: A Study of Love, Marriage, and Romance." Thousands have enjoyed and benefited from this series, which is available on videocassette and audiocassette. Both formats contain twelve thirty-minute teaching sessions and come with a study guide for personal and group use. This timely series is perfect for churches, Bible study groups, and individuals. Some people have even given it as a wedding gift!

For more information on:

- attending a Song of Solomon Conference by Tommy Nelson,
- purchasing the video or audio teaching series on the Song of Solomon, or
- purchasing other teaching material by Tommy Nelson

contact Hudson Productions at 1-800-729-0815, visit their Web site at www.thesongofsolomon.com, or write to them at 12001 North Central Expressway, Suite 150, Box 120, Dallas, TX 75243.